ON AIR

My 50-Year Love Affair with Radio

JORDAN RICH

With Stephen A. White

Foreword by Peter Casey

FOREWORD

Peter Casey
Former Director of News & Programming
WBZ NewsRadio 1030

I hear voices in my head. It is not as bad as one would think. During a long career people tend to pick up "skills" that are specific to their industry. Hearing voices in my head is one skill I learned as a professional listener. For more than twenty years I was Director of News & Programming for WBZ NewsRadio. I listened to those voices in my head and doing so served me well. I would be able to imagine the voice of a person or piece of music and instantly know that it is either a good fit (or a bad one) for a show or segment. Is the voice deep and rich enough for the mood? Does it *fill the radio with sound*? Would the lyrics and music here help or hurt the telling of the story? Those questions instantly rattled around in my brain and I would be able to give an instant thumbs up or thumbs down. One of the best friends and employees one could ever have was one of those voices. You might even be hearing him in your mind right now. It is the voice of Jordan Rich.

Five months into my WBZ tenure the day of October 29, 1996 started like almost any other fall day. I did not expect to be hearing Jordan's voice in my head. Sadly, our long-time friend and colleague had died in his sleep overnight and his daughter called to give us the unsettling news. Norm Nathan was WBZ's weekend overnight talk show host, working the midnight shift until 5am. My relationship with Norm was special to me, as were the overnight hours. The first job I had in radio was producing Norm's "Sounds in the Night " overnight program across town at WHDH Radio. Having been a fan and listener prior to landing this first media gig made me feel as if I had arrived in broadcasting. One program director at WHDH called Norm Nathan the best overnight man in the country. Eventually Norm was lured to another Boston station, WRKO, and began working with another young kid broadcaster going by the name of Jordan Rich. While dealing with our grief upon learning of the passing of Norm, we at WBZ had to process those feelings and then at the same time still do our jobs. I alerted the newsroom so the staff there could begin to cover "the news story" of losing our beloved Norm. I also had to determine how to find a host for the weekend overnight shifts. In a business that runs 24/7 there is no "down time." We were always on the air live. I needed to identify and hire a host to take over--either temporarily or permanently-- for Norm Nathan.

Jordan and I had met briefly during his time with Norm Nathan over at WRKO. Even though Norm had moved from WHDH over to the competition we kept in touch. I was always a big fan of Norm's wife, Norma, the *Boston Herald* gossip columnist. Earlier in 1996 Jordan had recently wrapped up a long and successful run as host of the morning radio program at WSSH. Listening to Jordan and Norm together on the air at WRKO I could hear the chemistry and similarities between the two. They had like senses of humor and easy-going interview styles; neither one was likely to reach across the table and throttle the guest as it often sounds on some interview programs. Whenever I thought of Norm Nathan on the radio the voice of Jordan Rich was also present. In my mind, the two were always linked. Norm's style was a good fit for the heritage that WBZ had built over the decades in New England Broadcasting. Jordan Rich has that same sense of on-air style.

By this time in radio's long history most radio stations had given up on maintaining a live presence during the overnights.

It is expensive and there are not a ton of advertisers knocking on the door to sell products in the middle of the night. Be it a music format, or talk, many stations had converted to syndication or voice tracking and saved the cost of keeping overnights live. We were fortunate that WBZ was committed to keeping it "live and local." Converting these weekend hours to something other than what Norm Nathan had built was never a consideration. We needed to continue that tradition and build on it. The overnight audience is made up of listeners that are more loyal to the hosts and the radio station than any other part of the day. They cherish hearing that voice in the night and if they do not like the host, they will let you know. I learned more than a few things at WBZ about the type of person that is a regular overnight listener. If you have ever driven in Boston during what we call a drive time commute you may have thought that the whole state is on the roads with you right now. Boston's reputation for horrible traffic is richly deserved and getting worse.

However, there are still thousands of people that don't do that commute, and many are regular overnight listeners. All have their own reasons for being awake for all or part of the night. Many of them sleep with the radio on just so it can be heard in case they wake up during the middle of the night. Others enjoy the quiet nighttime hours to get things done at home and prefer to sleep during the day. All have a different story for being up while most of the world is sleeping. One could assume that some are awake because they have trouble sleeping. Maybe some are depressed or lonely and just want company. It is a special breed. The overnight listener feels a certain entitlement and ownership of these hours. This mindset is like a foxhole mentality, a comfort zone, a place that is shared only with others like yourselves. Letters, phone calls, and emails from these listeners over the years illustrated to me that while this group is a collection of individuals they are also unified and do not want this time messed with by anyone. Any disruption or change to this status quo is met with immediate rejection of the new or different. The audience feedback will be swift. Ready, fire, aim. If I made even the smallest change or a programming element in the overnight show I knew the very next day listeners would be calling me and I would have to be prepared to defend my decision just as I would if called before a congressional committee.

It would be an embellishment for me to claim that I knew Jordan Rich would become the broadcaster he is today. When

7

asked by 'BZ's general manager what I planned to do with the weekend overnight shift I instantly answered that my first call would be to Jordan Rich. Norm's passing was only a few hours old. Conducting a nationwide search and research or focus groups was not in the cards. I brought up Jordan's name because it just came to me. It was a gut instinct call that was worth making. The result would be what any good employer could wish for when making this type of hiring decision. Take this job of replacing a legend and make it your own. Do not be a replacement. Make yourself irreplaceable. No one was more suited to be a steward of the Norm Nathan shift than Jordan in the weeks after Norm passed. The stewardship did not last long. It soon became obvious that Jordan would be his own man. Jordan was able to plant his own flag in the overnight ground. Norm was respected and is still appropriately remembered to this day. Jordan became his own legend.

Being a talk show host is a lifestyle. The role of a talk show host is to live your life on the radio. It is not something only turned on like a light switch or microphone switch. It is not comparable to the role of an actor who moves on to the next role, plot, and script. The talk show life must be lived and experienced and then shared with the audience to build any credibility and relationship with that audience. You are what you eat and as a talk show host you are what you read, hear, see, and experience. Jordan's life from the early years through his days as a young broadcaster and business owner contributed to a foundation. Experience hands us the ability to know we can withstand a storm in even the toughest of life and death situations. Jordan and his family can attest to that. A talk show host does not have to spill his/her guts out on every show to be authentic. A measured amount of sharing at appropriate times works more effectively and makes the listener want to know more. Always leave them wanting more. But the experience gained from daily challenges adds to the well of knowledge and can be dipped into when necessary. Jordan may not have shared with the audience all of the details of the tragic passing of his wife Wendy, his close encounter with fatality, or bouts of depression. However, the listeners still learned from it and received comfort and support from his experience. His wisdom comes from these life events and he can share his thoughts on these because he's lived through them and lived them out on the radio.

Experience can also be a voice in your head steering you in one direction or away from another. If you are lucky like I was you listen to the voice in your head as it guided me in the right direction during that fall week in October 1996. While the radio show for Jordan has ended, we can all still be enriched in the pages ahead from listening to the voice you will undoubtedly hear in your head. That sound you hear in the night is the voice of Jordan Rich.

INTRODUCTION
Why did I choose to write this book?

Ever wonder about the size and scope of the universe? I wouldn't suggest you do so. It might make your hair hurt if you spend too much time on it.

Over the years I've pondered a few of the big questions, as I'm sure we all have. But a long time ago, a "throwaway" comment by my junior high school science teacher caused me to pay a bit more attention than usual. Turns out the earth science class lesson that week dealt with the ionosphere and the ozone layer that encircled the earth. The teacher remarked that radio waves (I began to perk up at the mere mention of radio) travelled from transmitters to radios everywhere and then flew off into space, heading for—to quote Buzz Lightyear—"infinity and beyond!

I found it mind-blowing to think that a DJ in the Philippines, or a news announcer in Des Moines, would have their broadcasts beamed throughout our galaxy and whatever lay beyond—forever.

What does this have to do with my decision to write this book? Knowing that there is no end, no boundary that science can quantify, allows for mystery and magic, is a real turn on.

I'm fascinated by the prospect that there is more to fathom than that which we can see and touch. Radio waves are invisible yet we can prove their existence. Knowing that somewhere in the outer reaches of space, radio transmissions are accelerating and someday, perhaps already, may be heard by other species? There's awesome wonder in that prospect, an infinite sense of legacy.

But what about legacy, back here on earth? I've amassed enough recorded material from a 50-plus-year career to fill a wing of the Smithsonian. But I've never shared my life story in something as concise as a book.

So why now? Well, when AARP membership forms seem to arrive monthly and most of my contemporaries are now in their 60s (Oops, that means I'm there, too!), I figured it was time to put a few things down on paper as I best remember them. Thankfully, I'm still fit and trim and hope to live in good health for some time to come. But in the era of a pandemic, when health is a fragile commodity, why wait? I credit my wife

Roberta, who has the right attitude about not using the "wait until" excuse. Go for it now, she advises regularly.

I'm not a philosopher, teacher or counselor. Although I sometimes fancied myself somewhat of a "late-night radio talk show rabbi." No, I'm just an ordinary person hoping to elicit a few smiles along the way and perhaps an occasional pause on the part of you the reader. I invite you to reflect on the lessons I've learned through my many highs and more than a few lows.

As you move through the book, you'll read about the jobs I held at various radio stations in Boston, about the creation of my successful recording studio and voice-over business, and about mentors who have helped me move forward. I will also share personal memories, a few of which are decidedly painful, such as the long illness and eventual death of my first wife, and my dance with the "black dog" of depression/anxiety for several years. Interestingly, the chapters about me encountering rough patches come easier, recollections flowed more freely than I would have thought. It was somewhat cathartic to share these parts having lived with the experiences so intimately. Those events were like horrible neighbors who moved into my den, overstaying their welcome while wrecking my house. They had quite an impact.

Most agree that writing is a learning experience. If done with attention and care, it can bring serenity to the soul as one articulates his story. It has for me. But enough of the big picture stuff. I honestly wrote this as a gift to my children and grandchildren and as a primer for those embarking on a career in broadcasting. Hopefully a few of the lessons I've learned and the mistakes I've made will help others.

Finally, gratitude is one of the top meditative practices. That, along with empathy fuels my tank. But I can be long winded. If I were accepting an Oscar (a Walter Mitty daydream of mine), the band would surely play me off for going on way too long. So here is my short expression of gratitude. And for those I miss thanking, forgive me. I still love you.

To my family; my parents, sister Darlene, son Andrew, daughter Lindsay and son-in-law David, grandchildren Elle and Carter and, of course, Baby Dog. Your love and support mean the world to me.

To my late wife, Wendy, who fought so hard, loved life and never stopped caring about the rest of us.

To the woman who brought the gift of love into my life again, my wife, Roberta. I'm so grateful for you every day. And to my lovely stepdaughter, Stephanie, so happy to have you in my life."

To the mentors whom you will meet in this book, all fine people who taught me not only about the broadcast business, but helped me to become a better broadcaster and a better man.

To Ken Carberry, my adopted brother and comrade in 'tonearms.' Working with you isn't work at all. It's more fun than adults should be allowed to have.

To author and editor, Steve White, without whom this writing project would never have ever happened. He lit the fire while guiding me through the process.

To my friends and colleagues, too many to count, who bring meaning and connection to my life. I try my best to do the same in return.

And to those dreaming of using their creative gifts to make the world a tiny bit better: "Be Well, so you can Do Good."

Jordan Rich

TABLE OF CONTENTS

17

CHAPTER ONE

Thank You Thomas Sperry and Shelley Hutchinson

On June 6, 1944 the Allied Forces landed on the beaches of Normandy, France. Fourteen years later, on June 6, 1958, an equally momentous occasion occurred, at least in the Boston, Massachusetts home of Bernice and Marty Rich. That was the day I came into this world like most new born babies; making a lot of noise. And since I've been lucky to have been on the radio in one way or another for over 50 years, there are likely those who will tell you I never stopped making noise.

But any journey that covers over six different decades is bound to be a long, strange one, peppered with ups and downs, veering left and right, into happy places you'll always cherish, and dark places you wish you could forget. There was no GPS on this journey, no "recalculating" to help avoid the inevitable detours that life places in the way.

John Lennon wrote, "Life is what happens to you while you're busy making other plans." The legendary Beatle could have easily been my tour guide when I look back at a long career in radio. And it's a love affair that blossomed thanks not to Guglielmo Marconi, but to the unlikely duo of Thomas Sperry and Shelley Hutchinson.

In 1896, Thomas Sperry and Shelley Hutchinson established one of the most successful customer rewards programs ever known. It was the year the duo created the Sperry & Hutchinson Company (S&H) or, as it became widely-known, S&H Green Stamps. S&H sold its stamps to retail stores that would then give them out to customers as an incentive to shop at their store over a competitor's. Customers would collect the stamps, which ranged in value from one to 50 points, and place them in a book provided free by S&H. Once full, the book was worth 1,200 points and could be redeemed for just about anything, either at a local redemption center or through S&H's massive 178-page mail-order catalog. At the height of its success in the 1960s and 1970s, it was believed that S&H sold three times more stamps than the U.S. post office. And its reward catalog was the largest publication in the country. It was also estimated that 80% of American households collected Green Stamps during their heyday.

If you grew up in the 1960s it's hard to dispute that claim.

After all, who doesn't have memories of sitting around the family dinner table after the dishes have been cleared and getting to the task of filling those books with coveted S&H Green Stamps? Picture it, every night, millions of kids across the United States were spending time licking stamps, their saliva-fueled dreams focused on what great new toy they'd be able to get. And in the spring of 1967, eight-year old Jordan Rich now had his chance.

Walking into the S&H Green Stamps Redemption Center at 227 Parkingway in Quincy, Massachusetts with my mother and father, those treasured stamp books safely tucked away in mom's pocketbook, was like walking into Santa's Workshop. At this juncture, you might suspect my eight-year-old boy radar was zeroed in on any of the hot toys of the day. Would it be a Lionel Train Set? An Electronic Laser Jungle Target Gun? Or perhaps a G.I. Joe, complete with "action grip" so it could hold an assortment of "kid-friendly" bazookas, machine-guns, flame-throwers and hand grenades? No, something else had caught my eye that day, and when I saw it I knew it was worth every lick.

Before I reveal what I walked out of the S&H Green Stamps Redemption Center with that day, you have to also understand that I grew up listening to the radio religiously every night. But whereas most kids my age tuned into the popular disc jockeys of the day, playing those "platters that matter, the hits from coast to coast," I really didn't care that it was Judy's turn to cry (get over it). No, I was listening to talk radio, late-night airwaves filled with the likes of Larry Glick, taking calls from listeners on WBZ, the mega-watt radio station blasting out of Boston or from New York with hosts such as Long John Nebel. I reveled in hearing the chatter of Arlene Francis, the legendary Jean Shepherd (who brought *A Christmas Story* to subsequent generations), Barry Farber, who would later become a good friend, and countless other voices that skipped through the ionosphere.

Sometimes I would listen to ballgames from around the country. I was addicted to the CBS Radio Mystery Theater because it was just as it was billed—"Theatre of the Mind." My imagination was fully engaged as radio became my obsession. I imagined myself on the radio, hearing my voice coming through my battery-powered transistor, or the larger speakers of the family console. So, was it any wonder that this very happy eight-year-old walked out of the S&H Green Stamps Redemption Center with a Panasonic reel-to-reel tape recorder?

22

At last, I could hear what my voice sounded like on the radio (well, kind of). There was no stopping this young radio prodigy.

I set about interviewing my mother, my father and even my baby sister Darlene (who wasn't much of a conversationalist at four years-old). I also interviewed my grandfather who, instead or regaling us with tales of growing up in Russia, decided instead to tell some of his favorite cornball jokes to my microphone. I credit Papa Dave, along with my dad, for my rather dry sense of humor, very much based on puns and wordplay. But I didn't care if Papa Dave told jokes or not; thanks to my Panasonic reel-to-reel tape recorder I was on my way to someday being the next Larry Glick, Norm Nathan, Jerry Williams, Curt Gowdy or Lamont Cranston (kids, Google these names at your leisure).

So, I just want to say, Thank you Mr. Sperry and Mr. Hutchinson. It was all certainly well worth the saliva.

I'd have to say that 1967 turned out to be a pretty good year (especially if you were a Red Sox fan). Along with purchasing my trusty tape-recorder, it was also during that summer in the car with my Dad that I happened to notice a brochure on the front seat for the Northeast School of Broadcasting. The pamphlet had a big old-fashioned microphone on the cover. I was excited to find there was actually a school out there that *taught you how to be on the radio*! Could things get any better?

I held up the brochure and asked my father, "What's this?" He looked at me and softly replied, "It's nothing. Just something I looked into a while back. Never mind it." And that was that. To this day I believe that brochure was meant for me to see in my Dad's car.

Between the brochure and the trusty tape recorder, I was certain as to what I wanted in life. I have sometimes wondered just how much my dad might have accomplished had he taken the plunge into broadcasting. He was a fine singer and an amateur actor who certainly could have made his mark professionally, at least in my opinion. He had the looks, the voice, and the personality to be a fine entertainer. He even has a photo of himself and his boyhood pal, Leonard Nimoy (who hailed from Dorchester) when they appeared together on the TV talent show *Community Auditions* ("Star of the day, who will it be…"). And although they didn't win, Leonard Nimoy went on to fame as "Mr. Spock" on *Star Trek*, while my Dad became a successful accountant for a large hotel chain.

I owe my dad a lot. He introduced me at an early age to the Broadway classics, jazz, and classical music. He made me a James Bond fanatic by taking me to see *Goldfinger* in 1964, my first of dozens of encounters with Secret Agent 007. He introduced me to the Marx Brothers, Humphrey Bogart, westerns, Mel Brooks, and so much more. We continue to share stories about actors, radio shows, theatre and movies.

One of the great lessons I have learned, as a father and a grandfather, is the importance that parental pride can play in shaping the success of a child. Both my parents have always supported my career decisions. They went to every play and listened to nearly all my radio shows, even the commercials I've recorded. My parents have always *kvelled* (Yiddish for being proud). That has always been so gratifying because it's important to have people you love, and who love you, in your corner, especially when you go for something most people think is too darn risky.

CHAPTER TWO

High School: 'Readin', 'Riting', 'Rithmetic'...
and 'Radio

On a warm day during the first week of September 1972, I became a Blue Devil upon entering the front door of Randolph High School.

That summer had seen a number of noteworthy events, including increased bombing in Cambodia, the kidnapping of billionaire J. Paul Getty's grandson (who was eventually returned to his parents, minus an ear) and the death of martial arts master Bruce Lee, who I enjoyed watching as Kato on TV's *The Green Hornet*. At the same time I entered the hallowed halls of Randolph High School and things began to gel.

During the summer of 1973, and continuing through my sophomore year, TV and radio news reports kept up a constant barrage of information about the Watergate break-ins that occurred in June 1972. By the summer of 1973, investigations were in full swing, with numerous witnesses called to testify as the presidency of Richard M. Nixon hung in the balance.

During the drama of that summer I was riveted by news reports, on television and on radio. I studied the interview styles of many of my media gods; Dick Cavett and Mike Wallace, each of whom I would get to interview later in my career, local talk show hosts such as Jerry Williams and Paul Benzaquin, and, of course, the granddaddy of them all, Walter Cronkite. These were some of the greats who fueled my desire to sign up for the school's Radio Club.

But in 1973, during my sophomore year, I got a little sidetracked from radio by a fellow named Olin Brit.

If that name doesn't ring a bell, don't be embarrassed. Unless you breathe theatre 24/7, you'll not know who Olin Brit is. For those of us who do breathe "the stage" incessantly, we know Olin Brit as a member of the barbershop quartet in the hit Broadway musical *The Music Man*. It's a popular show with book, music and lyrics by Meredith Wilson, about a con man named Harold Hill who poses as a marching band organizer selling band instruments and uniforms to naïve Midwestern townsfolk, promising to train the members of the new band. However, he plans to skip town without giving any lessons, taking the town's cash with him. No matter how you size him up, Harold Hill is trouble (with a capital T, and that rhymes with P, that stands for pool).

In 1957, the show became a hit on Broadway, winning five Tony Awards, including Best Musical, and running for 1,375 performances. It has frequently been produced by both professional and amateur theater companies, including Randolph High School, where it was billed as the big spring musical production of 1974. It would be my first "real" role on stage, and I was both thrilled and anxious.

Even though I had never been on an actual stage before, I always felt the calling, putting on shows for the kids in my neighborhood. And yes, as a skinny high school sophomore with so much "experience," I thought I was pretty good. So, when auditions rolled around for *The Music Man,* I set my lofty sights on the plum role of Mayor Shin. I had put aside the fact that the actor who played the Mayor in the 1962 film (Paul Ford) was a rather tall, pot-bellied jowly character actor. I discovered after the auditions that the main reason I didn't get the role was because "I didn't exactly look the part." Instead the director gave it to a big kid, a seriously big kid, who looked much more like a 60-plus overweight political blowhard, complete with his own jowls. But I was cast nonetheless in another role, ending up a member of the production's barbershop quartet, which may have been helped along by the fact that my voice had changed (dropped like a fat lady opera singer on steroids into bass range territory) starting around the time of my bar mitzvah at age 13. I secured the role of the bass man in the quartet as no one else could get down that low without their voice cracking. "Lida Rose" and "Goodnight Ladies," became ear-worm songs (well before that term was in vogue). I worked hard on nailing my singing part on those two Meredith Wilson numbers. It was a harmonious debut.

I didn't really care what role I played; I absolutely loved it. I learned how to project my voice beyond the first few rows, about the need for stage presence, understanding how not to throw lines "up stage." I picked up on the technical stuff quickly, the blocking, or where and how to move, sight lines, scrim and other artsy terms, you know, like "wings" (not the spicy kind from Buffalo). I learned about diaphragmatic breathing, breathing from the core, using the full body for performance, breath being central to it all. That was one of the most critical skillsets that I learned at Randolph High. And everything I learned on stage would eventually cycle back and serve me well in my radio career.

The drama club at Randolph High School was very active and would produce not only a big annual musical but several one act plays as well. The productions were so well-received that very often we were invited to attend the prestigious Boston Globe Drama Festival competition. One of those selected one-act productions was Tennessee Williams' *The Long Goodbye*. At the time, it was considered a rather adult play, certainly not the kind of material most high schools presented. I played the Puerto Rican friend and wise cracking sidekick of the lead character. This is one role for which I absolutely looked the part! The lead in the play was my good friend Eddie Dunn, who was also the star—Harold Hill—in our production of *The Music Man*. Eddie and I became fast friends during the musical and we loved the chance to act together again. Truth be told, I quietly learned the Harold Hill role while watching Eddie do it. Not that we had them in high school, but I could have been his understudy. We had a blast working on *The Long Goodbye*. It was a serious drama about writers block, depression, economic hardship and sexual oppression. Since I wasn't nearly as "worldly" as I would be in say my senior year, there were elements in the drama that drifted a bit over my head. I remember a scene in which one of the characters opens his wallet and something falls out. Now remember the context, I'm young, innocent and not very sophisticated. At rehearsal, I had to react to this thing falling out of the other male character's wallet without ever knowing what I was reacting to. Was it a wad of gum, a cough drop, a book of matches from some hoodlum bar? Nope, I'm sure you've guessed it. The item in question turned out to be a condom. It took me the entire run of the show to figure that out. To be fair, a real packaged condom was only introduced at the final dress rehearsal. Prior run throughs featured a book of matches.

We rode that show through the regionals all the way to the competition finals in Boston at the old John Hancock building in the spring of 1974, and competed against some very high-end drama schools, such as Boston College High School (several of their students went on to have successful careers in theatre). It was thrilling to be on what was certainly the grandest stage in my young career.

Now, every thespian has his or her story, an odd incident that stands out from any performance. In *The Long Goodbye* in Boston, I had mine. I had the character down pat. We lived

31

together, Silva and me, He was my avatar for several months and I felt I could do the role, as most actors say, in my sleep. Well, sure enough, I remember vividly at one point during the play I had the uncontrollable urge to sneeze. And that is something no one should be around to witness, because I don't just sneeze once or twice and then move on. No, I've got to challenge the Guinness records for consecutive sneezes in one barrage (my record stands at twenty-six during peak allergy season). However, in successfully stifling the oncoming sneeze, I completely forgot where I was in the script. Total blackout, no touchstones, the set, Eddie, the lights, the audience, all suddenly out of focus. The line I was supposed to throw had me referring to a book (it had to do with the fact that Eddie's character was a struggling writer) called *Ghosts in the Old Courthouse*. But that line, in the midst of my panic over the itchy nose, was lost to posterity. Instead I blurted out in character, "God bless the Indians."

You might ask; where the bleep did *that* come from? Since those years I've done a good deal of personal and professional study on mind/body connection as well as hypnosis and the power of the subconscious mind.

Here is my theory on the origin of the wild adlib. Locals will recall at the time the Shawmut Bank appropriately enough had a proud Native American as their official logo. The bank was prominent and I distinctly remember seeing the picture of the Indian as the cast made the bus trip to John Hancock Hall and the theatre. So an Indian, the Shawmut Indian, was the image that popped in my head. Surprising as it was to me, the cast and the director whose blood pressure skyrocketed, the ad lib got a huge laugh from the capacity crowd. Tennessee Williams might be rolling over, but the moment secured me a spot in Globe DramaFest history. We didn't win first place at the competition but received several honors and production awards. Boston College High School won it all with a production of Jean Genet's *The Maids,* a play so adult in nature that it made our show seem like a 1950's sitcom. That school deserved every accolade it received.

Throughout high school I was lucky enough to play leads in most of the one-act plays. I also got to play the lead, Tommy Albright, (Gene Kelly in the film version) in *Brigadoon.* Mind you, I was not a great singer and certainly no Gene Kelly, but I learned to "talk/sing" and faked it rather well. I took cues from

Richard Harris, Rex Harrison and Fred Astaire. They seemed to have figured it out.

My favorite musical role in high school was by far that of Billy Bigelow in *Carousel*, the Rodgers and Hammerstein classic first produced in the 1940s. Billy Bigelow is a broad, boisterous carnival barker with a sizable ego and little care for others until he falls in love and ultimately expects a child. It's a complex enough role for an adult who has lived a little, let alone a high school junior (still not yet that worldly senior). The themes of responsibility, hubris, fatherhood and ultimately hope are expressed in such powerful iconic songs as "If I Loved You," "You'll Never Walk Alone," and of course "Soliloquy," a story-song solo that lasts close to ten minutes in which Billy contemplates what it will take to be a father to a boy, or perhaps a little girl. *Carousel* is a musical that has endured for so many reasons. Audiences react to the loss and pain felt by many of the characters, particularly Billy. They also respond to the closing scene that urges us to 'walk on through the storm.' This was the first time on stage I understood the impact of performance, not only to make them laugh. I had done that several times by now. That came easy. But *Carousel* introduced me to the broader emotional connections of love, loss and redemption. The parents, family, friends and Randolph citizenry laughed. Then cried. Then cried some more. Then stood cheering.

There are other distinct memories of my drama days in high school. I remember the time we went to the Globe Festival New England finals in Skowhegan, Maine. I remember it mainly because it was on this trip to Skowhegan where I had my first, shall we say, true experience, with a sweet young lady in the cast, at something very much unlike my style, a toga party! Clumsy, raucous, far from intimate but safely handled (thanks to my memory of the wallet prop from that earlier show).

Anyway, we racked up more awards, which I fully credit to the man who would be the first of several mentors, English teacher and drama club director Donald Nelson.

Donald Nelson was my sophomore level English teacher and directed *The Music Man*. He was quite theatrical and over-the-top, speaking in his clipped, meticulous pseudo-British kind of way, reminiscent of the character of Dr. Smith on the sci-fi TV show, *Lost in Space* (Jonathan Harris, who sounded so continental, actually hailed from Brooklyn).

Mr. Nelson could be very tough on his students because he wanted us to be good, to strive for excellence, to take part in the immense joy to be found in theatre. Most of us, not all, grew to love him, knowing how much he cared for us.

One example of his "tough love" was directed at me, a life lesson that I'll never forget. Very early in the rehearsal schedule for *The Music Man,* I chose to skip a rehearsal because I had a test coming up. Many other students in the chorus (my character was considered background) were cutting rehearsals, so I went along thinking missing one rehearsal would be no big deal. Here comes the life lesson. At the next rehearsal, Mr. Nelson took me aside and said, "We have an issue here, Mr. Rich. If you plan on skipping any more rehearsals I can pretty much guarantee that you're not going to be allowed back on that stage for the next three years of high school. If you don't take this seriously you're done!"

He was going to bench me for three years? No second chance, no pass? He continued, "I don't want you to turn into one of the 'monsters' that we have, with out of control egos. So either you play by my rules or you don't play." I never (and I do mean *never*) skipped a rehearsal from that day on. It was a crystalizing moment for me, learning the vital lesson that theatre is a team effort. Respect for others on the team is paramount. One should never think less of someone because they are hoisting lights or moving furniture; along with the actors, there are set builders, makeup artists, publicists and ticket sellers—all key people to any production. I witnessed students my age and older acting like prima donnas, and vowed to never go there. As a result, I had an outstanding relationship with the people on the crew, the "techies," because they knew I respected them, helping where needed or just staying out of the way. To this day I'm in touch with many of them and am grateful for their friendship.

Don Nelson contributed to my life and I'll never forget him. When I graduated high school he came to a party at my house and gave me meaningful gift—a portfolio of photographs that had been taken of me in every show I had appeared in since *The Music Man*. There were character action shots of me and my cast mates from nine different shows; pictures I never knew were taken at the time. He arranged them in a booklet with a personal inscription that I treasure. Years later, a bunch of us got together to throw Mr. Nelson a retirement party. He taught for decades and helped so many of us see the way forward with dignity, curiosity, effort and joy. I remember hugging him, both of us teary-eyed. He was approaching 70 at the time and told me how delighted he was to hear me on the air at WBZ. I was touched that I still made him proud.

Despite the accolades I received as a thespian on the Randolph High School stage, I knew by then that my future would involve a microphone

But how would I get there? And how would it begin? A woman named Nancy Boland Johnson provided the answers. Nancy was the coordinator of the Radio Club at Randolph High School, as well as the in-house PR director for the Randolph Public Schools. She was old school Brahman, sounding very much like a Beacon Hill resident; reserved, formal and conservative. Nancy was also a very talented writer and communicator and a woman of poise. As staid as she appeared in dress and tone, she was progressive and adventurous when it came to educating students about media. One of Nancy's tasks was to teach journalism, and she got me an internship as a cub reporter at the town's weekly newspaper, *The Randolph Herald*, covering school-related events (playground openings and bake sales) under the pen name Don Jay. I learned a lot from Nancy about style, effective writing and journalistic ethics. But her leadership in administrating the Radio Club was the spark that I needed.

Thanks to the Radio Club at Randolph High School, I graduated from interviewing family members to soon asking questions of politicians, athletes and celebrities. The experience of prepping and conducting an interview was exciting. As raw as I was, it wasn't long before I established myself as the "head guy" of the radio team. Of course, a big reason was that I couldn't get enough and worked as many after school hours as possible. I soon thought, "I can see myself doing this for a living. Absolutely!"

It wasn't instantly glamorous. One of the first interview opportunities took place in the school's janitorial office, with me asking probing questions about keeping classrooms clean, the infamous bucket brigade cleaning up unmentionable messes, and the scientific formula behind the famous soap-to-water ratio. It was a humble start to say the least. But once I "moved up" to interviewing the school superintendent, I could see a future for me in radio. And I thank Nancy for that.

Nancy also had a big old Ampex tape recorder that she would place on her conference table with several microphones plugged into a mixer. Then we would usher in the school department people, local town officials and, of course, our celebrity janitors. Nancy also had contacts with various entertainment facilities at that time (many of which still exist). Before long, we were traveling (tape recorder, note pads, and stopwatches in hand) to top venues in the area, asking questions to some of Nancy's favorites; stars from the Lawrence Welk Show and a host of big band and jazz musicians, including Count Basie, Stan Kenton and Guy Lombardo.

I have no doubt that in 1973-74, the other members of the radio staff would have preferred interviewing Don Henley or Bobby Orr rather than an orchestra leader (Basie) who defined the Big Band era of the 1940s. I, on the other hand, being a very old soul, knew these celebrities and their music and relished the opportunity. It was my chance to interview someone notable. We did several road shows, gaining backstage access and it was a hoot. Just when I thought it couldn't get any better, it did.

Nancy Boland Johnson had many contacts in the media and entertainment field (she passed away in September 2019) and among her accomplishments later in life was her weekly "Senior Set" column for *The Boston Globe*. She also had an "in" at WJDA, a radio station located in Quincy, Massachusetts. Each week Nancy would deliver the tapes of our interviews to

WJDA, for airing on Sunday nights. I am guessing that more people were watching *Mannix* or *McMillan & Wife* on Sunday nights. Few were huddled around their radio waiting to hear the latest Randolph High School interview on a 1,000-watt radio station. But *I* heard them. I could actually, for the first time, hear myself on-air on an actual functioning real radio station interviewing someone. As clunky and amateurish as they were, they were broadcasts. My radio "knockin' on the door."

One interview I fondly remember most was with Bill O'Connell, a TV sports reporter on the old Channel 5 in Boston. We were all excited because here was a TV guy who talked sports, which was hep and cool to the rest of the staff. He was patient and gracious with us, a bunch of school kids. Looking dapper in a camel colored leather jacket, Bill was engaging and really enjoyed himself. Bill also happened to be a very heavy smoker as many were back then. He coughed often during the interview. Bill succumbed some years later to illness likely exacerbated by smoking. His interview led to many others with local media personalities. The professionals we interviewed were happy to share insights; I learned a lot early on.

One last thing about being on the radio staff: there was an added perk, which was the use of Nancy Boland Johnson's private office bathroom. Trust me, that was a big deal. Like in those prison movies when the crafty crime boss gets privileges the other dumb schnooks don't. My own bathroom when I needed it was my privilege. I remember what high school bathrooms were like in the '70s; no doors, tiny individual squares of useless toilet paper, wall-to-wall cigarette smoke? Enough said.

I had a great time in high school. Made a lot of lifelong friends, had damn good teachers, a social life revolving around the RHS Drama Club, and got my first taste of what it would be like to have a career in radio.

All of this was in play as I applied to colleges; Boston University, Boston College, UMASS, all the usual local suspects. But it was a small college in Milton, MA that caught my attention. The school had a little 10-watt FM radio station. I found out I could join the "radio staff" in my freshman year, something that would have been impossible had I signed on as an Eagle or Terrier. So, I made my decision to enroll at Curry College. It would be the decision that would determine my life path. Most notably, it was a decision that would lead to meeting up with my best friend and future business partner, a relationship that is only getting stronger 45 years later.

CHAPTER THREE

College Days and Welcome to Boston Radio

In September of 1976 we were basking in the afterglow of patriotic fervor ignited by our nation's bicentennial celebration. I enjoyed watching what seemed like endless bicentennial broadcasts from Walter Cronkite, Harry Reasoner, David Brinkley and John Chancellor, all worthy candidates for the broadcasting equivalent of Mount Rushmore.

It was during the summer of 1976 that disco music first splashed onto the scene. And it was everywhere. A song by radio jock Rick Dees called "Disco Duck" made it to the number one spot on *Billboard Magazine's* Top 40 chart. High art for sure (however it did do more for aquatic fowl than the George Lucas' mega-bomb *Howard the Duck* film). Also on the movie front, in March 1976 filming began on Lucas' more successful venture, *Star Wars*. George was a smart cookie. In one of the most lucrative business decisions in film history, he turned down his directing fee of $500,000 in exchange for complete ownership of merchandising and sequel rights. Think about it; over the last 40-plus years every Wookie action figure, Hans Solo t-shirt, and Princess Leia hair extension that was purchased at sticker shock prices, ol' George got a piece of the action. May the financials be with you. Ka-Ching!

That spring, while Lucas began his path to riches in a galaxy very close to home and couples were practicing their dance moves to "Turn the Beat Around" and "The Hustle," I was undertaking the rite of passage known as the College Road Trip. Today, those road trips consist of air travel and hopping from hotel to hotel across the United States and beyond. It was a lot simpler back in the day. I stuck close to home, visiting the Boston biggies—Boston University, Boston College, University of Massachusetts—certainly venerable institutions of higher learning. But the one school that stood out for me was not a headline grabber. It was Curry College, founded by Alexander Graham Bell. Ring a bell?

Curry is located in Milton, Massachusetts, about 10 minutes from my home at the time. I didn't know much about Curry other than they were known for having a decent communications program and, more importantly, a radio station. It was a real honest to goodness, standalone radio station, complete with tower, transmitter, and a well-stocked record library. I found out during my campus tour, that unlike those more established schools, here freshmen could work at the station and I could be on-air in my first semester. The idea of having my own live radio show, something I dreamed about, sold me on Curry. Sign me up!

The call letters of the station were WMLN, named for the city of licensing, Milton, and not, as some cynical students coined it "WMLN---We Make Little News." It was truly a tiny college FM 10-watt station that lived—barely—at 91.5 on the dial. That meant on a good day, if the wind was blowing in just the right direction with perfect weather conditions, it might come in loud and clear a half mile down the road from the campus. But that didn't matter. This was my chance to work in radio with quirky students with pony-tails (men and women) wearing heavy metal t-shirts, torn jeans and in some cases dark shades day or evening, queuing up records, forgetting to shut microphones, taking meter readings, and ripping news copy off the Associated Press ticker. It was just as I imagined, complete with beer stains, cigarette burns on the carpet, and lots of horrid tasting coffee.

As I began my freshman year on staff at WMLN, upper classmen were tasked with teaching us newbies the ropes. And frankly, a lot of the learning we did was on our own, making tons of errors in the right environment. Mess up here; be better prepared for the professional world of broadcasting. We hoped.

Like most college radio stations at the time, the format consisted of block programming featuring different types of music (rock, jazz, reggae) and talk/information (sports, news packages, issue discussions, etc.). Well, being the kid with no experience as a disc jockey, the only shift available when I got around to the sign-up roster, was the classical music hour. And that was because, to put it mildly, classical music "wasn't cool."

The hip cats were playing hits like "Afternoon Delight" and "Love Will Keep Us Together". The "classics" of the day. Being a "glass half full" kind of person, I took the opportunity to learn something new and in the fall of *1976* signed up for the only air shift available, and soon began playing hits by artists with real staying power; Tchaikovsky, Wagner and Brahms, who hit the Top-40 Charts in *1876*. *Real* oldies but goodies. It wasn't a sacrifice because I did appreciate classical music and still do. Here's the best part of my very first live DJ experience.

By playing 20-minute long symphonies, in those days exclusively on vinyl, I would have plenty of time to prep my next master stroke at the control board. It was my methodical way to practice muscle memory and adjust to opening the mic, launching the next selection, queuing up the selection and running the control board. I wasn't doing the cool thing like the other jocks, playing two-minute-long top-40 songs. Those guys were quite stressed, losing their place, messing up transitions, tone arms akimbo. The upper classmen don't have much patience. The *cool jocks* were anything but and most could have used valium. Meanwhile, I remained calm learning how to navigate a radio show with "The 1812 Overture" cascading on for 15plus minutes. Plenty of time to plot my next move. I learned it all quickly in slow motion.

During my many years in radio, I've run many a board and take pride in having a steady hand on the stick. I have those early shifts with Wolfgang and Ludwig at WMLN to thank for it.

I was "King of the Hits from the 1800's" for a couple of semesters before moving up to the Department Head position of Public Affairs Director. A mere freshman and now I'm in management? Public affairs Director was a fancy title, but all it really meant was that I was the person in charge of putting public service announcements on the air and interviewing local community and college officials, similar to what I did in high school. It wasn't glamorous. But it did mean more responsibility. The FCC (Federal Communications Commission) back in those years required all radio stations (even the 10-watt variety) to air and log public service programming and announcements as a requirement for license renewal. Sadly, in my opinion, many of those rules disappeared during deregulation. Radio stations no longer have to allot time for public service. Many still do, but many regulations have disappeared.

Back to my first department head job in an office the size of a phone booth. I enjoyed the job, while getting to know the nonprofits in the area, creating produced announcements for the local YMCA, Women's League or blood drive. There was actual paperwork which I didn't mind much, but the most satisfying thing was the chance to interview again, sharing conversations that informed and hopefully entertained.

At WMLN we produced local talk shows. The issues-oriented public affairs flagship show was *RoundTable*. It was a hack

48

name, but we thought it hip and adult back in the groovy 1970s. It was at WMLN, while hosting and producing *RoundTable*, that I got to do radio with Kenny Carberry, who would become my closest life-long friend. We've been business partners for over 40 years, having much more fun than adults are supposed to have. Much more on our audio production business in an upcoming chapter.

Kenny and I ended up taking a lot of the same courses. The most significant of these were communications classes taught by another of my mentors, a professor of radio who taught us about the business and life, Roger Allan Bump. Roger, as he insisted on being called, was by day the News Director at WRKO, a powerhouse AM music station out of Boston. He was a Curry College graduate who worked his way up through "the tall grass" to a major market, respected and loved by generations of students and broadcasters.

By the spring of 1977, Kenny and I were working together quite a lot at the radio station. We were both commuting students, spending loads of extra hours at WMLN, working on our heavily accented voices, developing a love for both live radio and voice-over production. We each had part-time jobs, his as a stock boy at a local market, me as a busboy at an Italian restaurant in town. We're still known by clients and friends as "the boys." While most students only wanted to don shades and spin hot wax, Kenny and I worked hard to make the *RoundTable* show listenable and impactful. We hooked up with a local public relations veteran named Steve Allen, who worked with us to produce a series of radio programs with the doctors, nurses and educational staff at Carney Hospital in Boston, one of his key clients. Steve was a proud Navy vet, a big time chain-smoker and an active leader in the Dorchester community, a section of Boston. With Steve's guidance, we produced a long running medical series that went on to win a blue-ribbon award in health care communications. I remember a group of us heading to a downtown Boston hotel to accept the award. I realized then that radio has impact and the community appreciates the work we do. It was a proud moment. I've had many since then.

The other show that Kenny and I created, due to having so much air-time to fill, was a two-man comedy vehicle we called "Moondial." The show was basically a platform for two friends who shared the same zany sense of humor, heavily populated with puns and wordplay and references to movies, performers, politics and sports. He and I were simpatico. From The Marx Brothers to Bogart to Woody Allen and Mel Brooks, to Prairie Home Companion and The Muppets. To this day, the movie and TV quotes fly and there isn't a subject that doesn't result in a pun fest.

We did the show live for a couple of years but only ended up saving a few on tape. The elements were simple – two wise guys commenting on stories from the "National Enquirer" (our prime news source). We made up characters with distinctive shtick and would take turns interviewing each other. We did song parodies and brought on co-eds as "special correspondents" (a fine way to surround ourselves with girls). It was a poor boy's radio version of *Saturday Night Live*, without the stars, live audience or ratings. Lorne Michaels had nothing to fear from us. But it was somewhat popular on campus and Kenny and I had a creative playground to work out comedy bits. We bombed often. But as any standup comic will tell you, bombing is one of the prerequisites to future success on stage or on radio.

In my sophomore year I was promoted to Program Director.

Being the "PD" was a pretty big deal back then at WMLN. I got the green light to make changes to the format, one that had been in place for years. Up until then, it was top40 hits most of the day, pretty much free form depending on who was at the controls. It seemed like a good time to change things up. I didn't make changes alone. Kenny was right there with me (he would soon be appointed general manager at the radio station by the faculty advisors).

We started the "big switch" by signing on the radio station at 8:00am, instead of the noon hour. That ticked off a lot of the hung-over late sleepers. We then dumped the rock format and introduced a mix of jazz and big band music for the new start time. It was an effort to broaden listenership and attract some of the adult community in Milton, not just the Curry kids on campus. Kenny and I, along with a few other like-minded buddies, had the love of jazz in common and we had a ball with a show we called "Sunrise Serenade." Needless to say, there were some who didn't favor the changes. A small cabal took it to a nasty level, sabotaging our produced promos for "Sunrise Serenade" by dubbing profanity over the audio tracks. That type of tampering often results in fines and/or threats to a station's license. Oh, and to add to the fun, my tires were slashed in the station parking lot. All because a small group of "artists" were opposed to the changes we made. Follow up to that story? We caught the idiots (easy to identify their voices on the altered promo pieces) and justice was meted out. A satisfying ending.

Turns out the station did gain a small following in Milton proper, and we expanded block programming throughout the day to include a variety of music, talk and sports formats. This allowed students the chance to learn many facets of radio. Happy to note that in the 1980s, soon after we graduated, WMLN applied for and received a power boost and today is thriving as a full-time college/community radio station at 91.5 on the FM dial. It continues to serve as a superb training ground for future broadcasters.

Along with spinning records, writing news and handling the organizational duties that come with being a PD, I also learned how to edit the old-school way, using my eyes, ears and a razor blade. I owe so much of my early training (editing, mixing, mic technique) to the one and only Kenny. He's a natural at building and fixing things. Smart move to pick him as a partner!

I recall two ambitious projects we were involved in at WMLN. The first was an adaptation of a classic golden age radio drama, *Sorry, Wrong Number*. Some may remember the film version in 1948 starring Burt Lancaster and Barbara Stanwyck. WMLN obtained the 1943 radio play version by Lucille Fletcher. We did the production for two reasons; the love for old time radio drama and we had no budget. There were no rights fees to pay.

We had dozens in the cast, with Kenny and I producing, directing and taking a role or two ourselves. Everything was produced the old-fashioned way; no digital editing or easy downloads of sound effects. We became instant Foley artists out of necessity (Jack Foley was a sound effects artist in the early days of Hollywood who developed and shaped the technique of using everyday items to create effects. For example coconut husks on a block of wood to represent horses trotting.) It was slow, arduous work but loads of fun. Listening back to it 40 plus years later, *Sorry, Wrong Number* is a bit crude. But it was a major step forward, leading to a career in audio production.

Another fond memory was a promotion for charity inspired by our call letters M-L-N, nicknamed the *melon*. We staged a twenty-four-hour joke telling marathon, reminiscent of an old *Dick Van Dyke Show* episode. Kenny and I (with a few compatriots who filled in during our water and bathroom breaks) anchored the joke bonanza, telling thousands of riddles, puns and clean jokes (certainly a little innuendo here and there but mostly family friendly). It was exhausting trying to fill a whole day and night with just clean material! At the end, we were totally spent, barely able to whisper but we did raise money for a good cause *and* got coverage in a couple of local papers.

The promotion involved one of the station's sports staff, a lovable guy whom we set up to try breaking a Guinness Book record by eating as many melon balls as possible in a 24hour period. God bless old Rick. He did it and survived, although to this day I'm sure he wants nothing to do with a cantaloupe. WMLN was our radio playpen and launched my professional career. This brings me back to Roger Allan Bump.

Roger was a larger-than-life figure, a charming character with ties that never matched his jackets or shirts. He was the first adult I knew to wear clog shoes and be proud of it. He taught several communication classes at Curry, all involving life lessons about honesty, respect, preparation and care for the audience and colleagues. He'd often tell us, "Anyone can learn how to cue up a record or run the board. It's how you deal with the public and your colleagues that determine success in the business." He certainly taught us a lot about journalism, interviewing and how to best develop our voices. Roger would frequently invite local broadcast pros to his classes and I learned much from those lectures. He became a serious mentor as well as a good friend. He was also responsible for giving me my first big break on Boston radio.

Following the Great Blizzard in February 1978, WRKO made the decision to step up their weather forecasting game. Up until then it was a Top-40 radio station that did some news and added a weather brief here and there. But after that mega-storm *everybody* was talking about the weather. Roger was tasked with adding a weather component to WRKO's format, one that would not cost the station much out of pocket.

At that time, Roger had connections with the National Weather Service at Logan Airport, from which all weather forecasts originated. His idea was to place a news reporter at the airport alongside veteran meteorologists—middle aged scientists who wore flannel and lived and breathed isobars and storm fronts. Roger didn't want a government meteorologist calling in with a dry report. He needed someone with a pleasing voice and personality, who would get the information, credit to the National Weather Service, and report back to the station several times an hour during morning drive.

So, Roger, in his infinite wisdom, came up with the idea of having a student take on the job (there's your cost saving plan) and asked me if I was interested. "It's a great opportunity and I think you're the right man for the job," he said. "Would you like to do it?" I was stunned. Here I was a junior in college, about to graduate from 10-Watts to 50,000-Watts overnight. I couldn't have said yes fast enough. I was told to be at Logan Airport in East Boston by 5:00 the next morning. Roger had worked out the arrangement with the government weather honchos to allow me access. I couldn't wait to work in my first real professional studio!

The night before I barely slept, getting to the airport by 3:30am. I quickly found that the studio I dreamed about was actually a supply closet, complete with brooms, mops, slide rules and pencils. It did have a small table top and chair, as well as a station-supplied audio mixer and microphone. Luckily I brought along my trusty white ear-piece, the kind we used with transistor radios back in the days of Arnie "Woo Woo" Ginsburg on WMEX, broadcasting live from Adventure Car-Hop. My earwax buildup indicated significant use over the years. I was somehow set up to debut on "The Big-68, RKO!"

My task was to talk with the meteorologists, get the official forecast information, and deliver it in "WRKO style." We would record six to eight casts each morning. For the first few months I would arrive early, do my prep, record the casts and sit around waiting for a sneak thunderstorm to arrive. Whatever happened or didn't happen, I had to be on standby till 9:00am. Then I would leave for my first class at Curry, arriving with an early five o'clock shadow.

I encountered only one slight problem: the weather guys all seemed to hate me, or certainly the idea of a punk kid "looking over their shoulders and getting in the way." Who was this little guy coming in here stealing our thunder (pardon the pun)? I was stepping onto sacred ground, where no non-scientist had ventured. What to do?

Following the sage advice of my mentors, particularly Roger, I made it a point to develop a good relationship with them. I respected their skills and work ethic and stayed out of their way as much as possible, but paid close attention to ensure accuracy and detail. As time wore on I earned their trust, representing their work at gathering forecast data in an entertaining way on the radio, always presenting them in the positive light they deserved. Say what you will about government inefficiency, the National Weather Service (now the National Oceanic and Atmospheric Association or NOAA) is one of our most reliable, proficient public agencies. I would bring in fresh hot donuts almost daily. Never underestimate the power of a Boston Cream or honey glazed cruller. Cost me plenty but the results were sweet!

Before long, the station had me going live throughout the morning show. Some of the weather guys were quirky characters and they would wander into my little supply closet studio and I'd banter with them on-air. One weatherman, Mel, was a standout who could have had a career as a standup!

A meteorologist who I really came to know and admire was

Harry Turban, one of the original weathercasters at the NWS at Logan Airport. He also lived in Randolph. I knew the name, having heard him on the radio many times. Harry was extra nice to me because he knew my folks from the hometown. Others became pals and my respect and admiration for them grew over the years.

When I started at WRKO that spring, the morning DJ was Dennis Jon Bailey, a strapping country music Southerner who had a cool throaty delivery as he played the hits. DJB drank his fair share of bourbon back then and lived the disc jockey life style you've read about. So, one day he says to me, "Hey Jordan, you want to go on the air with me live and have a little fun?" To which I responded as always, "are you kidding? Say when."

My career as a Boston radio personality was about to take off. The jocks at the station would open my mic (they had the control over it, not me) so I had to monitor the show carefully, figuring out in my earwax-stained earpiece when the mic appeared open because (no surprise) they wouldn't give me much of a heads-up. I worked with several great morning jocks over a four-year period and few would prepare me for what was to come. I developed a reputation as a dependable ad-libber, able to quickly toss comebacks and punchlines, often in the voice of characters I created; my 80-year-old Jewish Uncle Max, Scotty from *Star Trek*, an English butler etc. I became very much a co-host on WRKO's morning show, broadcasting literally from a brook closet four miles away.

WRKO was a revolving door for morning drive hosts. I remember one time they hired a new morning guy touted as this super talent from out of town. He was there for about a week and one morning didn't show up. He had gone AWOL. So, I ended up hosting the show solo from the closet. The station managers knew I was the most familiar with the format, having worked with various jocks and been a consistent team member for a couple of years. So, they rushed an engineer into the Boston studio to hit the buttons and I assumed the role of remote host. "This is Jordan Rich, here to help you on the commute, a nice sunny day for you. And here's a song by Bread on 68 R-K-O." That was one of my favorite moments, weird as it was. Being on-air live under pressure is like no other adrenalin rush.

While at Logan from 1978 to 1982, I had the privilege of working at WRKO with several wonderful talents, including Mike Addams, a radio hall of famer who went on to work many years as an FM host, and one of the funniest, most creative comics and impressionists ever, Scott Burns, now a successful voice-over artist on the west coast. Then of course there was the nationally recognized radio legend Charlie Van Dyke, often heard filling in for Casey Kasem on American Top-40. But it wasn't until 1982 that I actually got to work in the WRKO building in Government Center in Boston.

Now it was the end of 1981. Music on AM radio was losing its luster. The format of WRKO switched from music to talk-radio with the station bringing in talk show veterans Jerry Williams, David Brudnoy and Dick Syatt. I was still part of the team... and still at the airport. Then one day Charlie Van Dyke (who by now was program director) had the idea to hire an established well-known local personality to host mornings. That personality turned out to be another of my radio heroes, Norm Nathan.

Charlie was considering bringing Norm over from rival WHDH and he asked me if I thought it a good move? I thought it a fantastic idea because I was such a Nathan fan. He has always been popular with the Boston radio audience. Getting the chance to know and work with Norm was exciting, assuming I'd still be on the team. Norm had hosted a show for years called "Sounds in the Night" on WHDH, where he would interview celebrities over the phone and play classic jazz.

Sure enough, Charlie invited me to "come out of the closet" and work at the station, side-by-side with my radio hero. Together Norm and I did the morning shift; 6:00am to 10:00am. The show was called *Morning Magazine* and it featured Norm at his wittiest, interviewing newsmakers, working his produced bits which were hysterical, all with me running the board, reacting to shtick and vice-versa. Norm was one of a kind, even when he nearly burned down the studio. He used to smoke a lot and ashes flew everywhere. I worked on the other side of the glass and one morning looked up to see nothing but thick grey smoke. Norm had flicked a few stray ashes, igniting his news copy. Thankfully, there were no injuries or serious damage, save the odor of stale cigarette smoke for about a month.

It was glorious working alongside "the old sport" Norm Nathan. We came up with a bit called "The Dumb Birthday Game" every morning at 5:30. Norm was amazed that I could

63

accurately recite the ages of celebrities and newsmakers on their birthdays. I read a lot and retain that sort of thing. I still impress friends with my knowledge of famous people and their ages. If we ever meet, feel free to challenge me.

Working with Norm taught me much. I learned the art and benefits of self-deprecating humor. Also, how to use just one dimension to enhance imagination. He understood the magic or radio more than most. I had a blast while it lasted. But as you know by now, in the mercurial world of radio, nothing lasts forever.

At the end of December 1981, WRKO decided to replace me with a new morning sidekick for Norm, citing my age and lack of experience, even though I had been doing the morning show for four years, remotely and in studio. But I was not completely off the team.

The new morning guy only lasted about eight months. And then there were more changes. Charlie Van Dyke liked me and the work I had done so he offered me a specialty music show on Sunday mornings. I named it "Music Sunday," a show featuring American standards and Broadway tunes. I was back to my music roots. I met and befriended many jazz artists and theatre folks who appeared on the show. One of whom was local radio legend Ron Della Chiesa, at the time host of "Music America" on the local NPR station. Ronnie remains a dear friend to this day. His memoir, *Radio My Way*, is worth reading.

I got married in June of 1982 and the new Program Director (Charlie had since departed for greener pastures) called to ask if there was any chance I could host the new Saturday morning talk show spot, starting on a particular date. I realized that would have meant cutting my honeymoon in Bermuda short by several days. But being a good soldier, and thinking here's a great opportunity for me to host my very own morning radio talk show, I said yes. So, we returned early. My late wife, Wendy, was so supportive of my pursuits in radio right from the start, I regret not having thanked her more often for going along.

I had hosted the show in August for a couple of weeks when they called me to say it's over and let me go. If you're associated with a format (I was with the station for over four years in its waning days as an AM Top 40 powerhouse) then standard operating procedure dictates you need to go, to be erased from the roster as though you never existed. It happens all the time, from top to bottom. Management doesn't believe in any long goodbyes. Rather, it is immediate exile.

Fortunately, I was prepared early on by Roger and others for the inevitable. And this would not be the last one by any stretch. The loss was stinging. It wasn't about the money; I was barely clearing a few hundred a week. I was suddenly kept from doing what I loved. But that is the business. You have to know that going in, and be ready to deal with it. Radio, for all its highs, can be fraught with disappointment. Here I was, only two years out of college, looking to help support a new marriage, and I was suddenly, for the first time, cast aside.

CHAPTER FOUR

Good Friends and CHART-ing a Course for Over 40 years

One of the big differences between high school and college might not seem significant, but I was a huge fan; you got to sit wherever you wanted. There were students who would only sit in the back row for every class (the same ones who head to the rear of the church), and some who wanted to be right up in front of the all-knowing instructor's face. I fancied myself a middle man; not so close that I might risk getting called on too often, yet not so far back that I'd need a hearing aid to catch every other word. As a newly-minted member of the freshmen class at Curry College in the fall of 1976, one of the first classes I enrolled in, which I eagerly anticipated, was entitled *Introduction to Broadcasting*, taught by the aforementioned Roger Allan. At that time, I didn't realize the impact he would have on my broadcast career and my adult life.

Grabbing an empty seat (squarely in the middle) that morning, I nestled in nicely with notebook and writing utensil, glancing around at the other students ("Hmm, fetching female college freshmen at 9, 10 and 2 o'clock"). Just as class was about to start, the seat next to me became occupied by a tall, skinny chap with a sharp chin and bright friendly eyes (reminiscent of Rob Petrie from the classic *Dick Van Dyke Show*). It didn't take long for us to strike up a conversation with a joke or two about this new experience—college. After exchanging pleasantries, peppered with some well-placed puns, he extended a large hand to formally introduce himself.

"Hi, I'm Ken Carberry. Call me Kenny."

"Hi, I'm Jordan Rich. Feel free to call me anything but Gordon. JR will do."

We found out that we had selected many of the same courses, including at least two broadcasting classes. It also helped our budding friendship that Ken Carberry was a fellow commuter. He lived very close to the campus in Milton and I was about ten minutes away in Randolph. Commuters then and now are a special breed. We lived at home, yes, but most of us worked part-time, owned our own cars and approached school as we would a full-time job. At that time, the student population was split down the middle between dorm residents and day timers. Today, it's rare to find students who don't live away at college,

68

even with a campus in the same city. I'm proud that I helped pay my way through school, having just as active a social life as those living there. Yes, I was part of the Curry lunchbox brigade with no regrets.

In getting to know Kenny, I learned he also did theatre at Xaverian Brothers High School in Westwood, Massachusetts, which quickly endeared him to me. That, and the fact that he was *begat* in radio, born, as he boasted, "on a turntable." Kenny's dad, the "original" Ken Carberry, is a highly-respected broadcaster. He was a male model for a time (dead ringer for Johnny Carson) and was one of the original Boston disc jockeys when top-40 radio became the rage. He adopted the radio stage name "Ken Carter."

Back in the 1960s, anyone with an ethnic sounding name (an exception being the one and only Arnie 'Woo Woo' Ginsberg) would need to 'WASP' it up so as "not to offend the masses." So, Ken Carberry became "Ken Carter" on air and soon moved onto management and radio ownership, ultimately launching Carter Broadcasting, operating successfully now for decades. Kenny's father was a dynamic industry leader then and now.

More importantly, he is like a second father to me, one of the most noble and well-meaning gentlemen I've had the honor to know.

As younger Ken and I got to know each other during those first few weeks, sharing our love of radio, the Red Sox, *Young Frankenstein* and *Star Trek*, it turned out that Roger Allan, our professor, knew Ken Carter quite well. As a result, Kenny's dad would end up guest lecturing in our class on more than one occasion. A solid set of radio family connections was quickly available to me. And as we grew friendlier, Kenny would invite me over to his house in Milton, where I got to know his Dad and Mom and the rest of the Carberry siblings. I'm quite lucky to have been "adopted" by my Irish extended family.

Kenny and I began working together at the radio station in our freshman year and haven't looked back. He was spinning folk and hillbilly songs on a show called "Country Comfort," while I was the "classy one" in the joint with my Mahler, Mozart and Mendelsohn mixes. Eventually, we did it all; everything we could wrap a microphone cord around. Remote broadcasts, interviews on the fly, breaking news shows, sports talk, production of promos and public service announcements, formatting and more.

Through it all, and up to the present, Kenny and I crack each other up—a lot! Rarely does time go by without a quip, a set up and punchline, and usually a groan-inducing pun. The gags have flown daily in the studio, on the phone, via text or email, and out on the road during our "gig" days.

For over 25 years as mobile disc jockeys on the gig circuit we spun records and hosted over two thousand events – weddings, bar mitzvahs, reunions, christenings, a bris or two and even the occasional memorial service! Never a dull moment. Like the time a soused uncle danced and crashed his way into our speaker system. Or when asked by a prankster nephew to play the "Anniversary Waltz" for a couple celebrating their 50th only to discover that the wife was legless and in a wheelchair. I must have spent interminable 30 seconds, to the horror of the family crowd, begging the couple to dance, even for a few moments, to a few bars from "The Anniversary Waltz." Or the time on a Boston Harbor cruise when one of the overly-served rowdies decided to jump ashore before docking only to wind up in the heavily polluted waters of Boston Harbor. Or the time we worked a reunion when the power went out. Luckily there was a piano. Kenny and I switched things up in a hurry playing

"Name that Tune" and our own version of "The Dating Game."
We killed it that night by candlelight.

It's always interesting how decisions you make early on determine so much of your life's path. Had I chosen to attend Boston University, with thousands as opposed to a few hundred fellow students, it's likely Kenny and I would not have met. And all would have been very different. But we did each opt to attend a small set-in-the-suburbs college, a profound choice that set us up for quite a ride. But I'm getting ahead of myself.

Despite not living in a dorm, we were for all intents and purposes living at WMLN round the clock. We frequently took our gear out to cover events on campus, interviewing students, coaches and professors and the occasional big name such as consumer advocate and presidential candidate Ralph Nader, who once lectured at Curry. We produced and hosted comedy shows, toiled over an endless loop of analog production spooling through miles of tape, edit blocks and razor blades, and we played records... *lots of records*. CD's hadn't arrived yet which is all you have to know about the time period. We loved it all – developing and hosting shows, writing copy, crafting new formats, creating character voices. Kenny is blessed with a flair for radio engineering. With his dad so involved in the business, he got into wiring, soldering, dials and tone arms at a very early stage. He taught me everything I know about editing, multi-track recording, mixing, and helped us transition smoothly from analog to digital production back in the mid-1990s. Kenny is the technically gifted one— me, not so much. My contributions have always been on the writing and performance end; I leave the designing and building of studios up to him. There is no one better.

In 1978, as juniors at Curry, we decided to venture out on our own to make a little extra money. Venturing out wasn't hard; making any money, however, was. So we did pro-bono public service announcements for a couple of local agencies, using our voices and talent to gain any amount of traction as a legitimate production group. Anything to get experience and build a portfolio. We were a couple of big shots in a very small world. Kenny and I dressed similarly and conservatively, old-school button-down Brooks Brothers. We share the same conservative political views and values, remaining open minded and respectful of those with differing opinions. He's a Catholic of deep faith; I'm an observant Jew. We don't take ourselves too seriously and therefore feel comfortable and grounded. I've mentioned some of our shared passions. The greatest one is radio.

In 1978, we decided to form our own mobile DJ company. DJ's were all the rage during the height of the Disco revolution. We purchased turntables, speakers the size of coffins and enough music from local record stores (raise your hand if you miss Strawberries Records) to be dangerous and set out to conquer the dance floor.

Our first official gig was a disco dance at Randolph High School, my alma mater. It's all about who you know. One of my high school teachers remained in touch with me over the years and when he found out I was in the DJ business offered us our first show.

On a humid Friday night in the spring of 1978, Chart Broadcast Services was born. The payday was impressive back then: $100 for four hours of groovy hits and some mic work, in a four-way split. A whopping $25 buckaroos per guy, enough to sport a decent dinner with tip at the local Howard Johnson's. What's this about a four-way cut? I failed to mention there were originally four of us who embarked on the DJ adventure. That's how the name Chart came about. The "C" stood for

Carberry, the "R" from Rich, and the "H" and "T" for the other two guys. Two fine fellows David Hemenway aka "Mr. Shmay" and Jay Trotsky who ultimately didn't want to continue on the road, so we parted as business associates. But we all remained friends. So, Chart Broadcast Services launched in 1978 with that disco-heavy Randolph High School gig. Kenny knew how to get the equipment to work of course. I tried my hand at emceeing the affair, aping whatever famous disc jockey I could think of doing so questionably. I knew little about the music of the day, having never been a pop fan. Ironically, I learned quickly about pop, rock, disco, amassing a collection of thousands of songs. When we stopped "gigging" in 2000, I stopped paying attention to pop. Back to jazz, classical and soundtracks.

In those early days on the road, our DJ'ing expertise was sketchy at best. We had a cringe-inducing logo of a blue lightning bolt on our business cards and stationery. One big record-spinning cliché!

In the spring of 1980, as we were getting ready to graduate, Kenny and I decided to put together a real business plan. I was working at the time at WRKO for very little money. It felt like the right time to chart our own course (pun intended) and incorporate. Unlike some entrepreneurs who borrow so much up front they can never dig themselves out, we built it slowly utilizing a balanced, cost-efficient strategy. We did everything on the cheap.

We began by "borrowing" studio time from radio stations in return for us offering our voice-over talent. Our first client was Ira Olds Toyota, a car dealership north of Boston. A friend of Kenny's dad had a small ad agency and gave us a shot to produce our first spot. That fine gentleman was Joe Goldman, a fast-talking nut with a heart of gold. Years later Kenny and I were DJ's at Joe's son Garry's bar mitzvah. Garry remains a dear friend and colleague, as does his dad. Relationships are gifts; I've been blessed.

We wrote our first spot with multiple characters and a storyline which the client liked. The radio spot, our first foray into theatre of the mind, featured clowns, balloons, circus animals and a brass band. I was the announcer who declared Ira Olds the place to buy your next car (sounding more like 'caahhh'. I hadn't yet excised myself of my Boston accent, a lifelong pursuit). Listening back to those early creations is a reminder that you're only as good as your last performance. Thankfully with time, we all improve.

Kenny and I could see it was going to start slowly, but we made it our goal not to go into debt. We spent whatever we had, paying as we went. While broadcasting daily on WRKO, I was still bussing tables on weekends at the local Italian restaurant in Randolph. At the same time, Kenny was working as a stock boy at the supermarket in Mattapan. .

We each were raised in upper middle-class families and were endowed with a healthy work ethic. Long days or long drives didn't deter us from pursuing projects and generating work. Frankly, we made very little money, certainly not enough to sustain any kind of reasonable lifestyle, at least for the first two or three years. We cobbled it together never thinking to ask for help financially from our families. We had a simple goal. Find clients anywhere we could and build a reputation for quality production.

We eventually found work through various contacts and connections. Our first state-wide public service campaign was for the Massachusetts Chiropractic Association. Chiropractors back then were looking to improve and legitimize their standing with the public and they chose a radio campaign to do it. Other early clients included an organization that promoted Bible reading and three clients who have been with Chart since the

77

early 1980s; Sullivan Tire and Auto Service, The Boston Symphony Orchestra, and the Massachusetts Bar Association. A pretty prestigious group of clients on paper, but it was several years before our income matched any prestige.

During this time, we hired ourselves out as voice-over talent and reached out to friends in the industry whom we could count on as freelancers. But we needed to generate more cash, aside from occasional commercial production and weekend record hops. So the idea of us teaching what we knew about the voiceover business made sense. There weren't many places offering training in the art form and despite the fact that we were still pretty new at this, we did have our share of experience. Again, thanks to "who we knew around town," we landed teaching stints at the adult education centers in Boston and Cambridge, which proved to be fulfilling and profitable. It became a staple over the years. With both group and individual coaching, we've helped hundreds of people launch careers as voice-over artists. Teaching is one of my most rewarding pursuits. I was mentored by wise, kind and giving teachers and so appreciate their guidance. Helping others to learn is a natural extension.

We did a lot of writing and still do, taking cues from *The Dick Van Dyke Show* model. I'm sure you remember Rob Petrie (Kenny's lookalike) and Buddy and Sally, with walk-ons by prissy producer Mel Cooley? In the Chart Productions writing room, one of us would pace (always Kenny), while I pounded away at the IBM Selectric—controlled chaos with both of us tossing around scenarios, characters, slogans, adspeak and jokes. Back then it was a non-stop barrage of puns and joking, all the while chugging coffee and running short of Wite-Out. Same for today, except with better coffee and spell-check (no need for correction fluid).

By late 1981, we had enough work coming in to erect the first official Chart recording studio, renting office space in the same building as Kenny's dad (WROL Radio) at 312 Stuart Street in Boston, three floors above an elegant Boston dining establishment known as Flash's Snack and Soda Shop, across from the equally elegant Greyhound Bus Depot. We joined forces with Kenny's sister, Joyce, who was a graphic designer and did some voiceover work for us, and a one-man agency run by a short, mustached, middle-aged adman named Howard Temkin. Howard had a major retail account, a company called Ski Market, with several northeast locations selling skis and equipment. We ended up working with "Howie" for many years and had loads of fun along with our share of screaming fights over the "creative" of Ski Market radio spots. Ski Market was a solid account that paid us well for several years. We used those high-profile spots which ran in many markets to garner new business. Kenny conceived of and built the studio and I pitched when I could. We were so proud of our first studio in our own workspace on Stuart Street in downtown Boston. As the business started to expand, we required a bit more room and moved over to Boylston Street across from the Boston Common. Our intent was to stay close to the advertising agencies in Park Square. This area was the core of the Boston advertising mecca, where nationally prominent companies like Arnold Advertising and Hill, Holliday, Connors & Cosmopulos were headquartered. In 1995, we moved again in the same general neighborhood into the Statler Office Building at 20 Park Plaza, our final Boston address.

Funny story about that move. Always looking to save money, we decided to forgo hiring professional movers and do the job ourselves. I volunteered to hire a van from U-Haul in Framingham where I was living at the time. Framingham was about 30 miles west of the city. It was an easy assignment; drop down the company credit card and drive the van to the old office to pack up the gear for the move. One slight hitch. The van turned out to be a truck, a big one. And it wasn't equipped with automatic transmission.

It was too late to nix the deal. There were no automatics available when I arrived to pick up the truck. "You do know how to handle a standard?" the U-Haul attendant asked. He might as well be asking, "You do know how to do brain surgery, right?" As usual I answered in the affirmative. Embarrassed and up against the clock I said, "Sure, I can handle a stick."

So I took to the Massachusetts Turnpike determined to figure out just how to do it. Step on clutch and then shift. How hard could it be? Well, I'm sure I burned the clutch out on the vehicle, chugging along in first gear doing 30mph down the Pike in a 65mph zone. Stopping to pay the toll was unlikely. I slowed down enough to throw several dollars at the toll taker. I made it to Boston somehow and everyone waiting for me enjoyed a good laugh. And I learned a valuable lesson; leave the truck driving to the pros.

This was also about the time when significant changes occurred in our little business. In 1993, I bought my first desktop computer. Hard to believe but prior to that time I did everything by hand, banging out scripts and invoices on a typewriter. I entered the computer age learning from scratch about copying, pasting, folders and documents. That was step one in the evolution. The second step came two years later when we made the switch from analog to digital recording. Analog recording of course meant tape, razor blades, and a lot of clunky but reliable gear. The change to digital audio was a must at the time and with Kenny's help I adapted quickly. We could compress audio and send clients' commercials instantly via the web. Chart Productions went from hiring bike messengers several times a day to one-button delivery online. Sad for the bike messenger company, but a high-speed development in efficiency for our industry. We got up to speed quickly and currently use the latest recording and conversion software to increase our output of material substantially.

The one constant, the thing that hasn't changed over all the years, and will never disappear, is the human element. You still need to have the artistic talent and writing skills to create effective commercials, narrations, and sound design. What you don't need is as much infrastructure or overhead. With high-tech advances, came more changes in the industry. The big powerful heavily-staffed ad agencies in the mid-to-late 1990s began to dry up as clients realized that they didn't need to be paying as much to get the job done. Companies created inhouse marketing departments or chose to deal with small, cost saving boutique agencies. The kind of lean and effective operation we had always offered was now in more demand. Part of our decision to move the studios out of downtown Boston had to do with convenience. When the commute got to be too time consuming and expensive (especially during the Big Dig era, which made every commute feel like the Bataan Death March), when the rent for downtown office space began skyrocketing, and when it cost as much to park each day as it did to feed a small family, we made the decision to pack up once again and this time head to the suburbs. So, in 2005, with a touch of sadness we left the city behind and moved to our present location in Braintree, Massachusetts, not far from South Shore Plaza, one of the oldest shopping malls on the east coast. I was back in the old neighborhood, with Randolph being just minutes up the street.

After a few weeks, with a much-improved commute, new modern workspace, less of a rent burden and FREE parking, I knew we made the right move. Soon, clients and students wanted to come by again without the hassle of city traffic and parking costs. It was and continues to be a good fit.

As I look back over 40 years, I recall standout moments with some interesting people along the journey. Being situated near Boston's Theatre District, I got to meet and interview lots of famous actors, comics, writers and more. There was a lot of celebrity traffic through our office in those days. Tony Randall stopped in to promote an *Odd Couple* reunion with Jack Klugman. There he was, Felix Unger in all of his glory, looking dapper in our office. Tony revealed to me the fact that he was color blind and owned 30 or so blue blazers along with 30 pair of grey slacks. Another favorite memory was meeting prolific character actor Charles Durning (*The Sting, Dog Day Afternoon, Tootsie*), who was in town to record a quick public service announcement. The former WWII decorated soldier recorded the script and ended up hanging with us, drinking coffee and sharing movie stories for most the whole day. Another brilliant performer who stayed the entire day was political satirist Mort Sahl. After we taped the interview, he settled in for the long haul (about seven hours), regaling us with humorous stories including some about former presidents that should remain locked in the National Archives.

Then there was Theodore Bikel, who was starring as Tevya in *Fiddler On The Roof.* He dropped in for an interview to promote the show and told us he was starved. How could we say no to the poor milkman from Anatevka? So we offered him bagels and cream cheese, and he moved in with us for a day. One of the sweetest people I met was Liza Minnelli, an absolute doll. One might think she'd be a bit diva-like or at least challenging to interview. Quite the contrary, Liza was kind, self-deprecating and grateful for our conversation.

They weren't all enriching experiences, however. On the other end of the spectrum was legendary Irish actor Richard Harris, who was coming through Boston as King Arthur in a production of *Camelot.* He was in his 60's by that time, crusty, angry and without a doubt feeling no pain; a nasty unlikeable curmudgeon. At the press conference he treated the publicist and the people around him horribly and was very touchy about anything we asked. None of us who were there to interview him that day walked away feeling good about it. Two things to say here. The way any one of us treats those who serve us –

waiters, drivers, security guards–it tells you a lot about a person. Those who bully don't garner my respect, nor should they. At the same, as challenging as it sometimes is, I try to separate the artist from the art. I appreciate Richard Harris for his depth of talent and the joy he brought to me and millions in so many film and stage roles. I do also cut him and others in his position some slack. Alcoholism is a horrid disease, a personality blocker. He no doubt was masking pain. Still, it's never a reason to mistreat others when they're trying their best. The craziest individual I've ever met by far was movie star Mickey Rooney, who made one of the greatest entrances ever at a press conference, sliding down the marble banister at the majestic Wang Theater in front of me. It had to be at least 50 feet of staircase to descend for the cherubic septuagenarian, in town starring in a production of *Sugar Babies* with another Hollywood icon, dancer Anne Miller. Mickey was great fun, but totally zany. He could pose as the original poster child for adult deficit disorder. It was Andy Hardy on steroids. Don't know the reference? Just me showing my age.

Being in Boston, we of course came into contact with a number of star athletes. One of our colleagues and good friends, Steve White, (whose name graces the cover of this book) was the PR guy for an upscale condo and apartment residence called Charles River Park near Government Center (their slogan on a well-placed sign became a city fixture, "If You Lived Here, You'd Be Home Now") and there were a lot of athletes living in those apartments due to its proximity to the old Boston Garden. One day in the fall of 1995, Steve came in to cut a radio spot for Charles River Park bringing with him the Boston Bruins' Adam Oates and M.L. Carr, a great former basketball player who at that time was the General Manager of the Boston Celtics. They had a ball recording a spot together and both were a delight to work with. True gentlemen. We've had the pleasure of working with and recording scores of players and managers from all of Boston's pro teams and the takeaway for me is always the same. These men and women perform remarkable feats on their fields of play. We mere mortals admire them from our stadium seats and daydream about doing what they do. When the same stars come by to perform in front of a microphone, they are on our turf and are often humbled about letting us guide them. To be able to share tips and mentor famous performers from any field is exciting and satisfying. Reminds me of another tale, also sports related.

Back in the mid-1980s we were working for the Red Sox, producing radio spots to promote ticket sales. Chart got the work thanks to Kenny, who had been working summers at Fenway Park as a control room operator (programming the scoreboard in center field) and as legendary PA announcer Sherm Feller's backup. At the time, I was morning host at WSSH-FM when the Red Sox invited me to join several other morning show hosts from competing radio stations to a pregame hitting contest, on the field, the hallowed one where I watched my heroes play, Fenway! The chance to step on the field, to hold a bat, walk to the plate and take a swing where Yaz and Ted and Fisk did? You're kidding, right?

The game was scheduled two weeks hence; having not played more than a pickup softball game or two in the last few years I took to training, heading to local batting cages for many hours of practice. My nerves were on edge. Would I embarrass myself, would I even make contact, or get the ball out of the infield?

The big day finally arrived. I had practiced, psyched myself up watching baseball movies, I even took selfies (Polaroids) of my swinging technique. Can you guess what happened? If you're thinking the penultimate scenes from *The Natural* or

Field of Dreams, you're a bit off the mark. Think THE scene in *Singing in the Rain.* Sure enough, it poured for three straight days, the game and needless to say the pre-game contest was washed out, never to be rescheduled. My one chance was whisked away from me by the angry rain gods. My bucket list still includes stepping out from the seats onto the field at sacred Fenway. I'd be happy with that, no need to even hold a bat in my hands.

The overwhelming numbers of people I've interviewed have been exceptional, something I credit with some modesty, to the fact that I connect well with folks and manage to get them to relax. People share so much in common. Family, food, hobbies, aspirations, fears, hopes and humor. That doesn't just extend to celebrities but to everyone. I love my work for many reasons, with the connections and relationships I've developed being high on the list.

We have worked for years with prestigious organizations such as the Massachusetts Bar Association and the Boston Symphony Orchestra /The Boston Pops. For 25 years I've come to know and grow friendly with Boston Pops conductor Keith Lockhart. Kenny spent some time with multi-Oscar winning movie composer and Pops Emeritus Conductor John Williams.

Together we've interviewed dozens of musicians and stars thanks to our association with the BSO. One of our longest-running partnerships has been with Sullivan Tire and Auto Service, a regional family owned and operated company. Their time tested motto is "we treat you like a member of the family" and, trust me, there is truth in advertising in this case. They are dedicated car care experts, take exemplary care of their employees and practice ethical corporate leadership. I am so very grateful to Paul and all of the Sullivan Tire family for their loyalty and friendship over the decades.

In 2020 we celebrate the 40th anniversary of Chart Productions. Kenny and I still have things to learn about our changing industry. We've had a running joke for decades; that it only takes us four years (and it's always *four* for some reason) to catch onto the next big wave, to figure out where the industry is headed and to make moves. I'm happy to report that we've caught the best wave in a long time and this time we're not four years late!

Business has improved substantially thanks to podcasting. Chart is producing and hosting dozens of podcasts for a variety of clients and we're lining up new business regularly. I've hosted my own podcast, "On Mic with Jordan Rich," now since

2018. Radio on demand is on fire and for two veterans who began in the analog age, producing podcasts (which to us is all about radio content) is squarely in our wheelhouse.

Sure, like most other businesses, we've hit bulls-eyes and have missed some along the way. But through the ups and downs of economic recessions and evolving trends in radio, advertising and production, there has been one constant – Kenny and I have been together. We are still a solid team with a friendship based on brotherhood, family, loyalty, honesty and sharing in so many interests. Like a long married couple we often finish each other's sentences. We are mega *Star Trek* fans (Classic Trek from the 60s is our go-to) and share a love of jazz, reading, Sinatra, James Bond films, and sci-fi, as well as higher pursuits such as The Three Stooges, Mel Brooks, Larry David and standup comedy in general. I'm Jewish and he's Catholic. We often joke about our ethnic backgrounds, finding humor in most everything.

Back to the incredible characters we've met. As mentioned, Kenny worked at Fenway Park for many years as the backup announcer to Sherm Feller. I got to know Sherm well in his later years. He was the very first radio talk show host in Boston in the 1940s, wrote a thousand songs (as he used to say, "999 of them were flops") and if ever there was a Damon Runyan character come to life it was Sherm Feller. He "knew everybody," from the Cardinal of the Archdiocese and the top mobsters in Boston, to Nat King Cole and Ted Williams. Talk about a connection to the golden days of show business and sports! His stories were classics and we often talk about the fun he brought to our world. Note: often impersonated by die-hard sox fans, my impersonation has been voted #1 by those who knew Sherm best.

Kenny and I remain very close. He was best man at my first wedding (to my late wife Wendy) in 1982, and that same year I was an usher at his wedding to his beautiful Mary. We are also unofficial godparents and uncles to each other's children and grandchildren. Kenny's mom had five kids of her own but always referred to me as her "other son."

They say it's rare to be best friends and terrific business partners. Ours is a relationship based on love and trust, on having each other's back. Always. He has never once been envious of my on-air accolades or public attention. It's always been 100% support. And that support extended to times when it was really needed, including my grudge match with depression that you'll read about in the next chapter. He and all of the

Carberry family was a beacon of comfort when Wendy struggled with cancer, finally losing her battle.

How many businesses can boast of celebrating their 40th anniversary with the same two goof balls at the helm? Not many I'd guess. There's no mysterious secret to it. Since the beginning we have split everything, all profits, right down the middle 50/50. We rarely disagree and truthfully have never raised our voices in argument. We're loud enough as it is! After all these years we are still "The Boys." I've been given a great gift, to work with my very best friend. Two kindred and kooky souls who share much and would do anything for each other. Just another reason to be so grateful.

CHAPTER FIVE

When You WSSH Upon a Star

It's a phone call nobody wants to get; your boss calling to say, "We're making some changes." That was pretty much the message delivered by Mel Miller, the program director at WRKO that warm August day in 1982. Adding to the sting, it came on the heels of my agreeing to cut my honeymoon short so I could host some Saturday morning shows. Mel thanked me for my loyal service, saying the station was making the change to talk radio. They wanted to unveil a "fresh sound with fresh new faces." So, after five years at WRKO, and married barely two months, I was out of a job.

I had been in the business long enough to know that no radio job lasts for long and some stations change formats more often than others. Nevertheless, it was painful. My new bride was furious, "How can they fire you over the phone?" I told her it happens all the time in the business and as soon as you're gone management sweeps away any evidence (promos, posters and any digital remnant) that you ever appeared on their roster. Thankfully listeners, the folks who really matter, remember.

I figured things would be bumpy for a while. We were living in a Natick apartment with my wife, Wendy, teaching in nearby Hudson, MA. The only steady work I had was with Chart Productions, which was growing slowly in the early years. But I knew I wanted to get back on-air, to return to live radio—with Peggy Lee's "Is That All There Is?" An earworm too tough to shake. I thought, "How do I come back? What if I can't."

Things started to brighten up a bit in October of 1982. Chart Productions rented office/studio space above the elegant Flash's Snack and Soda on Stuart Street in Boston. Because we needed additional income, we sublet a bit of our space to a gentleman named Steve Chartrand, the Sales Manager for WLLH and WSSH, two regional radio stations licensed to Lowell and Lawrence, MA. I had a convivial relationship with Steve, respected his work ethic and the success he was having with his AM-FM combo of stations. One day over coffee he mentioned that WLLH had a talk show at 6pm weeknights and the fulltime host was leaving; would I be interested? This was only a few months since my unceremonious exit from Boston radio. I thought it over carefully – for about 3 ½ seconds—and agreed to take it without fully contemplating the logistics, namely travel and time. But I felt I had to get back. I loved being on-air and didn't think it would help my career to stay out too long. How ironic that my return would have me hosting a talk show--- after being canned for not doing talk!

I was getting paid little at WLLH, all the while fighting rush hour traffic to get from downtown Boston to Lowell, about 50 miles. But the opportunity offered a chance to hone my skills in talk radio, as my aspiration had always been to host my own program. I found myself working just such a gig on a small 5,000-Watt station in the Lowell/Lawrence region at 6:00pm, smack dab in the middle of the dinner or 'suppah' hour as we New Englanders say. A talk show with barely a phone call. The perfect boot camp training ground. Oh there were a few diehards, or "regulars" you hear calling in to most every station and I had a few I could depend on.

I recall one of the more colorful ones was known as "Moscow Mary." She was literally a card-carrying dues-paying member of the Communist Party. God bless Mary, she got the phones jingling with her anti-America rants. There was also the loveable middle-aged loner we nicknamed "The Brando Man." He worshipped Marlon and knew and loved everything about old movies. He would call regularly and I really took a liking to him. He was such a sweet guy with so much movie knowledge that I invited "Brando Man," (real name Harold) into the studio from time to time. Years later, when I was hosting the overnight show at WBZ, I asked "Brando Man," to guest host with me one night. He called it one of the happiest times of his life. Sadly, he passed away a few years later, but when he did, many listeners wrote and called to offer condolences. He, like so many in the wide wonderful audience, was a valued member of my growing radio family.

Hosting the show in Lowell forced me to learn how to gracefully ad-lib, often for hours. Storytelling in the form of monolog is a valuable skillset. But the raps need to be organized with arc and flow, all while coming across as conversational. Again, I learned from the radio masters whom I listened to avidly – Norm Nathan, Gene Burns and David Brudnoy in the Boston market; and such icons as Barry Farber and Jean Shepherd, nationally.

To ensure flow and content, I would book guests—city leaders, local writers, entertainers—as each broadcast sharpened my interview skills. One learns early on that a winning talk show is never based on the number of callers in the queue. It's the much wider listening audience that matters. Stats indicate that less than 1% of the audience is at all interested in ever calling a show. Even in the Lowell radio market, ratings were tabulated and we had decent ones during the 'suppah' hour, with folks tuning in regularly to hear topics of interest.

For a welcome break, once a week I hosted a show called "Tuesday Night Trivia," two hours of coasting. The calls would pour in with the lines jammed 10 minutes before airtime. We would reward trivia winners with extravagant prizes (dollar scratch tickets, coupons for fries at the local Mickey D's) and everyone and I mean everyone loves the idea of winning something from a radio station. Norm Nathan used to joke that "coming up folks, the next five callers will win whatever is in my trash can and I'll throw in a pen cap and some paper clips!" His way of de-cluttering his messy office!

On some *TNT* shows, Kenny would drive up to co-host with me. There were other colorful characters joining the trivia panel, including Brad Shepard, the talented WLLH morning host at the time. Brad was a fine actor and impressionist and we would often perform dueling Bogarts or Groucho and Chico routines for an appreciative audience. The show was unscripted with puns and one-liners flying. Since I fancy myself a fan of trivia with a passion for film, TV and history, I felt right at home. Most weeks our stomachs hurt from laughing.

The Jordan Rich Show was airing live on WLLH Monday through Friday. Here was a show of my own where I could experiment and learn about pacing, interviewing, countering callers who disagreed as well as disagreeable callers. From the start I committed to treat the audience with respect and kindness, never to bully or to let the title of host go to my head. Roger had taught us from the beginning to live by the original FCC code—to broadcast in the public's interest, convenience and necessity. Life lessons about being gracious, empathetic and non-judgmental as much as possible were my guideposts.

The WLLH show was working, but it turned out to be a short run. The time it took to get there and back and the extra prep on top of my work at Chart was a challenge. I wouldn't arrive home until 9:30pm or so, eating dinner by 10:00pm, almost always alone. Wendy would greet me and have to head off to bed to get up early to teach the next morning. This was "dues paying time" and I understood about sucking it up. But I was also a newlywed and we weren't seeing enough of each other.

Wendy, bless her soul, was always patient and understanding despite my schedule.

Station management appreciated my dedication and the way I handled things at WLLH. After several months, they offered me a weekend slot on their sister station, WSSH-FM. The WSSH studio was in the same building as WLLH, creepy enough to warrant an address such as 1313 Mockingbird Lane. From the outside, one would expect to be greeted at the rusty steel door by Herman Munster. It was a rundown factory building in the downtown section of Lowell that was still years away from revitalization. The place was cold, dingy, dusty and downright spooky. The homeless would build early morning bonfires in the dumpster by the main entrance. Inside, much of the paint was chipping, the rugs were torn, the smoke from the elderly receptionist's three-pack a day habit settled in like thick LA smog in the hallways. The FM studio itself was the size of a tiny walk-in closet. A far cry from the ultra-modern downtown WRKO radio facility. But all that aside, what made WSSH a logical choice for me that one extra day a week? There were actually 50,000 reasons. I started my pro career working for a 50,000-Watt Boston station, lost that to regroup again at WLLH which pumped out 5,000-Watts. Let's see, not that I'm a math whiz, but I was down a full zero. Now I was about to add that zero back! It meant that on Sunday afternoons, for six long hours, I was back to broadcasting to northern Massachusetts, parts of New Hampshire and, more importantly, to Boston and points south and west. People outside of the Merrimack Valley would rediscover Jordan Rich. Whatever happened to that guy, anyway?

The format of WSSH at the time—in 1983—was "soft adult contemporary music," which meant the songs of Neil Diamond, Barbra Streisand, Chicago, Luther Vandross and The Little River Band. Actually, it meant *a lot* of Neil Diamond, Barbra Streisand, Chicago, Luther Vandross and The Little River Band. To this day, when I am at Fenway Park and hear "Sweet Caroline" (a Red Sox rally song for some unknown reason) I have a mini PTSD flashback of my days in the closet playing endless Neil Diamond records.

So here I am, working Sundays at WSSH, weeknights at WLLH, and weekdays at Chart Productions. As for married life, my wife would not have been surprised to open the refrigerator to find my picture on a milk carton. I realize now, hindsight being a gift, that I was pushing way too hard, was apart from

Wendy too much and would have done myself a healthy favor by saying no to a few things. The radio business has an addictive hold on guys like me. The adrenalin rush of impacting an audience for me is intense. I felt it on stage at Randolph High School and I get the same charge when performing today. Only in my "golden years," have I been willing and able to turn things down, back off for more important reasons; family, physical health and inner peace.

Broadcasting now as a jock from WSSH was a new adventure. I got back to running a control board again, an activity I enjoyed. What I didn't enjoy was the long commute, now six days a week. I was constantly in transit back then, logging at least thirty thousand miles per year; a true road warrior. One weekday afternoon on the way to the station I played the odds with the needle near empty and found myself stuck on the side of the road, completely out of gas. I felt like a jerk as my little Honda sputtered to a stop. Remember, there were no cell phones back then so it was put the flashers on and wait. I figured I'd be late for my shift, breaking the cardinal rule of radio – you must show up on time! Incredibly, who should pull up behind me in the breakdown lane but the station owner's wife, with a full can of gas to help me on my way. She never let me live that one down. I still wonder how she knew it was me and why she would be motoring around with enough emergency gasoline to power a fleet of semis.

WLLH and the talk show only lasted for about a year when in late 1983 they offered me a full-time gig at WSSH. They wanted a livelier more engaging host to take over the morning show. The current announcer had a distinctly "beautiful music" style. Not his fault; it was what the previous format called for. So I became a "morning man" again at WSSH 99.5 FM, and was excited about being back on a 50,000-Watt radio station with reach and a relatively hip format and a growing audience. However, it did come with one unusual condition.

What I wasn't told when I accepted the morning post was that the fellow I was replacing wouldn't be going anywhere. The plan was for me to slide into the host position while the gentleman who had been the sole captain of the ship for years would pivot to the number two role as newsman, second banana, and sidekick. If you're thinking that doesn't sound like a healthy idea, knowing anything about show business, bullseye! What made matters more complex was the fact that said gentleman (first name Bill) had his share of idiosyncrasies.

Let's just say his ego was legendary and he didn't take kindly to criticism, let alone demotion. Remember I wrote how they axe you in the radio business, erase your name from the masthead and move on? This was the one radio station in America that decided to buck the system and retain the talent. This meant a dicey transition for me, working with him daily, learning how to placate and soothe the savage beast. I was his enemy and it took months of labor on my part to break through and convince Bill that we could make it work. Interpersonal conflict resolution was not part of the job description. But make it we did. We were a team for nearly 10 years. It helped to have my self-deprecating sense of humor working for me as well as curiosity about what made Bill act the way he did. I did turn into somewhat of an armchair psychologist as my effort to understand and work with him had everything to do with our success.

For the 13-plus years I was at WLLH and WSSH, we moved to different studios a number of times, usually coinciding with new ownership. In the late 1980s, the latest owners decided to move us out of the soon to be condemned haunted mansion in the Merrimack Valley to a new industrial office complex known as Cummings Park in Woburn, MA. We moved into a much nicer, cleaner workspace with state-of-the-art studios. Three years later in 1991, we were sold again and this time moved to Soldiers Field Road in Brighton, MA, a section of Boston, just across the street from the legendary AM powerhouse WBZ, the second oldest commercial station in the country. Everybody in New England knew WBZ. I imagined what it might be like to ply my craft there ... someday.

For well over a decade I worked for so many different program directors, general managers and owners it is easy to lose count. There was one standout, a guy I really admired. His name was Chuck Morgan and he had bounced around in various markets, enjoying success in many of them. Chuck was a warm, gracious, caring boss who respected the on-air staff. He was demanding but understanding. A true mensch. He ended up moving his family to my town of Framingham, living just a few streets away from us. For his short stint, the WSSH jocks had a leader we respected and supported. That is until the corporate knives came out and Chuck was let go. It happened to a lot of quality people back then, and it still does.

Glowing reviews for Chuck; I can't say the same for others we worked with, some who were in my opinion "certifiable" or on the wrong dose of meds. Trying to placate petty, resentful managers was a full-time exercise in survival, but necessary. Some were easier than others to negotiate. On a few occasions, I was moments away from throwing down my headphones and walking. WSSH was a non-union (SAG-AFTRA) station and despite strong ratings, we were vastly underpaid compared to the rest of the market. We had little if any leverage or bargaining power. One set of owners threw the talent a bone, offering incentive contracts based on ratings. Bonuses were promised and after one strong ratings period when we scored small bonuses, management rewrote the contracts, *moving the needle* on those incentives. We were dejected and angry. I remember inviting the full-timers to Chart Productions one evening to talk it over. We realized we risked losing our jobs if we did fight. So we ended up taking the rewritten deal. They had us by our mic cords.

Despite some rocky moments, I had a fulfilling run at WSSH, especially with on-air colleagues who remain my friends. As the morning show evolved with the station gaining traction, I introduced more personality to the show, interviewing many celebrities who visited the studio on promo tours. They included Tony Bennett, Daryl Hall, George Carlin and two favorites, Linda Ronstadt and Harry Connick, Jr. Linda was in town promoting her new Latin music album. She bore little resemblance to the beautiful young girl on roller skates from the 1970's album cover. It didn't matter to me, she was delightful. Harry strode in wearing a white t-shirt and jeans. We hung out over coffee talking about *When Harry Met Sally*, Sinatra and, of course, New Orleans. I was surprised at how tall a dude he is; a solid 6'3" and ripped. Harry stayed longer than scheduled and we hit it off well.

At WSSH, music was the Holy Grail. As a jock, you had to stick 100% to the playlist of carefully selected, exhaustively researched songs. And for the most part we did, knowing the consequences of playing a song out of order or dropping one for time. It drove us crazy playing the same songs over and over. You can't tune out when you're the DJ. You are forced to hear EVERYTHING. A playlist of 400 songs on a 24-hour rotation? That's more than anyone's fair share of Air Supply or Kenny Rogers. I occasionally bumped heads with programmers over the selection and repetition of music, but rarely did things get heated. Rarely.

One memorable incident occurred when legendary radio personality Jess Cain, a staple of morning radio for 40 years and one of the most talented, creative performers in Boston broadcasting was about to retire with one final show on WHDH. I took 30-seconds at 8:20am to acknowledge how special this man was to radio, congratulating him on a remarkable career. That was the extent of it. Well wishes to another of my radio heroes, whom most breathing members of the audience knew and admired. As soon as my shift ended, I was called into a closed-door meeting and scolded for acting stupidly, risking the loss of thousands of listeners who would be turning the dial to WHDH to hear Jess, leaving us in the dust because of my ignorance and disloyalty. The Program Director continued assailing me and accused me of being "amateurish." I was seconds from storming out in defiance. But self-discipline kicked in. I hung in there taking the abuse but refused to apologize.

I always respected the audience, never assuming them to be lemmings. Sadly, many of the programmers and consultants I've known do. Radio listeners are for the most part decent, hardworking people, who are bright enough to figure things out for themselves and can spot insincerity easily. The idea that taking 30-seconds to pay tribute to a radio legend would prove harmful was inane. Instead, it represented camaraderie among competitors. What I would hope colleagues from other stations might say about me someday. My arguments to the seething PD that morning fell on deaf ears, but I'm damned proud I did what I did.

A few days later I heard from the man at the center of the controversy. Jess Cain called to thank me for my kind words (somebody out there was listening) and complimented me on MY show! That brief call led to a warm friendship with Jess that lasted until his passing in 2008.

My overall experience at WSSH was positive. I did a slew of remote broadcasts and dozens of personal appearances as the WSSH lead personality. If there was a stage with an audience large or small, I was there. Ringmaster at any number of circuses, emcee for concerts at the Boston Garden, hosting major charity auctions. I remember introducing Barry Manilow at Great Woods and hosting the Longwood Tennis Tournament for several years. I brought Judy Collins up on stage at Symphony Hall, narrated pieces with the famed Boston Pops and one year in front of 20,000 screaming kiddos at City Hall Plaza had the distinct honor of introducing Barney the Purple Dinosaur (truth be told he was such a big star back then that backstage interaction was not allowed. A dictum straight from the reptile's handlers).

They weren't all glitzy red-carpet events however. I played my share of "smaller venues." I'll never forget the time they had me appear at the opening of a paint and wallpaper outlet in Peabody, MA, 10:00am on a Saturday. There was no formal program. My assignment was to appear in one of the aisles with a small WSSH banner to welcome shoppers. I met four people and a couple of dogs. Aside from the pooches, only one person responded with a hello in return. Turned out the wallpaper buying crowd wasn't much of a crowd. When has it been? I thought, "This is silly. But I'm getting paid for two hours, so count the minutes, hand out bumper stickers and continue to smile." Like the great punchline, "What, and give up show business?"

Note, I was doing all this while getting up at 3:30 in the morning, working until 10:00am, then heading over to Chart Productions until 5:00pm or later, all while being a young father, trying to help my wife raise our two kids; Lindsay, who was born in 1987, and Andrew, who came along in 1992. The whirlwind pace was not without its downside. A bit of darkness would set in. Stay tuned.

During the WSSH morning show, I got to be a little creative, resurrecting some of the characters I developed at WRKO. I would record one portion of dialogue as my characters (an old uncle from Florida, a South Boston truck driver, an effete Boston Brahmin) and play the lines back so that I, Jordan the affable morning host, would be conversing with these characters in real time. It required prep and spot-on timing with all of it performed live, no net. Often, I would bang out a script while a song was playing, inspiration coming from whatever was going on in the news that morning. Was it all comedy gold? Surely not. But I'm happy to report no tape ever jammed and no animals were injured during production! I owe the inspiration for these bits to a mentor. "Talking to myself" was one of several classic routines from the imaginative mind of the late Norm Nathan. Thanks, Uncle Norm.

In radio, change is constant. Whenever something is purring along pretty well, some consultant who needs to justify his existence, suggests changing things up. One big change to my WSSH role occurred back in the late 1980s, when management

111

thought it would be a super idea to team me with a female partner. "Boy-Girl" shows were popular back then. They made the decision to bring in Lesley Palmiter, a popular rock jock at WCOZ in Boston. Lesley is a very lovely person, and I am friends with her to this day. Unfortunately, arranged marriages in radio don't always work. Our on-air chemistry really never clicked and she was let go in a little less than a year. I felt sad because we worked hard to make it gel. It wasn't her fault. She was expected to blend in seamlessly with a new and different demographic. Not easy to do, especially in Boston, one of the hardest markets for even natives to crack. Things just didn't work out for Lesley and WSSH management. In just a few years, they would stop working out for me as well.

By the winter of 1995 new management had taken over again, and they weren't running the station very well. Morale was low and there were rumors of a major format change coming. They weren't pushing any new promotions or keeping the format fresh with new music. The station felt stagnant; there was little communication with the staff and the feeling was all too familiar, that a blowout was coming. Most everyone realizes that in radio if you're going to get whacked it's going to happen right around Christmas.

I had the strong sense in December of 1995 that I'd be the last man standing when they did unload just about all of the on-air staff by Wednesday. I was certain that my final show would happen no later than that Friday. Knowing I was a dead man walking and the format was about to flip, I broke the golden music rule to play a few tunes I had always wanted to play, Sinatra's "My Way" being one of them.

I got off the air at 10:00am and as expected got summoned the General Manager's office to hear, "Would you please close the door?" Here it comes. The manager, a forgettable glorified ad salesman if there ever was one, told me I was "an awesome" employee, one who had given so much and my value was off the charts— oh, and you're fired! They simply had to let me go to clean house. I asked him what was ahead for the station (by now word had leaked) and he said they would be switching on Monday morning to the latest rage to sweep the nation, a smooth jazz format. It was going to take the city by storm, replacing WSSH, a solidly rated adult contemporary format for over a dozen years with thousands of devoted listeners. On Monday, folks would be treated to a non-stop stream of John Tesh and Kenny G. music, or as the departing air staff called it, "a slow and syrupy kiss of death." I was saddened and angry on the inside, 13 years coming to such an abrupt end. But I thought of my mentor Roger Allan, who reminded us to never to burn a bridge on the way out. Opportunities will arise and the way one exits the scene says a lot. I kept my composure, even when told that my severance would cover a measly six weeks, a big thank you for working 13 years without a sick day. When asked why so little in severance, the answer back was as cold as a freeze pop, "You're lucky to get that much, seeing we are new owners and have only had this place for a year. We're not responsible for the previous 12 years." What a sweet send off.

A few days after my latest firing, I got a call from Susan Bickelhaupt, a reporter for *The Boston Globe*. She asked me to comment on what happened and I told her that the switch in format was not unexpected, and that it was surprising that they wanted to change from what was a ratings success to something untested. I added that the only regret I had was not getting a chance to say goodbye or thanks to the audience for their support over the years. To me, the quotes seemed respectful and rather harmless. Apparently, management didn't see it that way. The honcho who took pleasure in shoving me out the door on Friday had actually offered to pick up the tab for a small "disappearing from the dial" party for me, but when he read the

Globe piece it was summarily canceled, remaining staff were ordered NOT to attend. Three or four from the station bought me a drink at the local watering hole anyway. Brave of them for sure.

Looking back, the reason the honchos were so rattled had less to do with my quotes and more the overall tone of Susan's column, which was less than complimentary about the format change to smooth jazz under the new call letters WOAZ ("The Oasis"). The station's program director at the time, Bill George, was very high on the switch, and was quoted in the column as saying, "I told our sales staff that it's like if you're used to going to McDonald's every morning and the next day you go to Legal Seafood." Hmmm. It said a lot about what they thought of the substantial WSSH family audience so carefully cultivated by us over the years. It seemed to the new regime that the old audience was the "Happy Meal" crowd, beholden to fast food eaten with one's fingers. And when Bill George was quoted that WOAZ would be highlighting key artists such as the aforementioned Kenny G., the reporter suggested that many cringe at the thought of that kind of music. Context needed here. The new station died a quick death in less than a year. It was sold again at reduced value and soon became the dial spot for WCRB, a long-time classical music station.

Additional context. Kenny G. (real name Kenneth Bruce Gorelick) is an accomplished Jazz sax player who has sold millions of records. Stations overplaying his hits led some to turn away from his work. I interviewed Kenny a few years ago and found him to be engaging, self-deprecating and a real maven of jazz. Never judge a musician by his album cover.

So, the end of my FM run came and I walked out of the station for the last time with head held high, the bridge untouched by flame. As I walked to the parking lot, there staring right back at me was the building I had glanced at every day for four years; the complex housing WBZ AM 1030 and her sister TV station WBZ Channel 4. Not to mention the famous tower that was brought down during a major hurricane in the early 1950s and rebuilt to stand tall to this day. There she was, the radio starship of Soldiers Field Road, a legendary station that has been on air since 1921. And I thought, "Boy, would I love to just get one more shot at radio and maybe work there...just for a day." High hopes.

For the next six months or so I worked at Chart Productions as I always had, making calls, sending out aircheck tapes and resumes, reaching out wherever I could to see if someone would hire me to join their air staff on a part-time basis. Few returned my calls and those who did had the same message. I was talented and a good guy but too associated with the old WSSH format. Having a radio presence somewhere for years was akin to wearing a scarlet letter. "We like you, but you're not a good fit." Even though I re-invented my persona a few times during my career, it appeared I was right back where I started. I might have realized my dream to be a Boston broadcaster, having it come to a hard stop in my late thirties. It was a frustrating period. Then, in September of 1996, I took a phone call that would change things up in a big way.

"Hi Jordan. This is Bill Flaherty over at WBZ. Do you remember me?"

Here I am at
5-years old,
reaching for the
stars as the first
Space Cowboy!
(1963)

At 13, modeling my bar mitzvah suit and pretending to be Roger
Williams at the piano. (1971)

My first role on stage in Randolph High School as Olin Britt, bass voice of the barbershop quartet in *"The Music Man."* I am the handsome guy in the middle. (1973)

My favorite role as Billy Bigelow in *"Carousel."* I might have been the skinniest guy to ever play the part. It was during that show I learned how powerful theatre could be. I would make the audience cry. (1974)

119

At Curry College working with Ken Carberry at WMLN. Our future was decided in the era of rotary phones. (1977)

Jordan Rich

New Englanders love hearing about the weather. They revel in reports about the heat and humidity, and sneer at the first sight of snow. But from what source do they hear the weather reports? From the 68RKO "Weather Source," of course! 68RKO is "The Weather Source," and Jordan Rich is at the heart of the source.

My first professional radio gig as weather reporter for WRKO in Boston. Dig the '70s porno mustache! (1978)

Interviewing the great Tony Randall. He was indeed quite neat.
(1981)

My WSSH-FM publicity photo.
(1985)

Clowning around at a charity event with my daughter, Lindsay. (1991)

Wendy and I during happier times. (1995)

Presenting an award to WBZ talk host Dr. David Brudnoy. (1995)

With Kenny meeting and interviewing Roger (James Bond) Moore (1998)

Raising money on air for Children's Hospital. (2004)

Doing my
late-night
radio show on
WBZ.
(2005)

124

Papa with two
who light the
way; my
granddaughters,
Elle and Carter.

Sailing the
Caribbean with
my beautiful
wife Roberta.

CHAPTER SIX

Close Encounters of the Near Fatal Kind

Many years ago, when discussing whether or not a particular politician should take on the press, someone a lot smarter than I coined the phrase, "Never pick a fight with someone who buys ink by the barrel." And to that I would add; "Never pick a fight with someone holding a sawed-off shotgun to the back of your head."

It was a pleasant Thursday morning in October of 1992. Everything about the day seemed mundane. The local football team was 0-5 under quarterback Scott Zolak (about the same time a 15-year old Tom Brady was lighting up the football field at Serra High School in San Mateo, California), and Clint Eastwood's *Unforgiven* was racking up box-office dollars and accolades in the press, on its way to a triumphant night at the Oscars.

I had signed off at WSSH at 10:00am that day and 20 minutes later was pulling into a strip mall located off Montvale Avenue in Stoneham, a suburb north of Boston. It was like a hundred other strip malls dotting the state back then; a nail salon, dry cleaner, pizza joint, maybe a Radio Shack. And it's not too much of stretch to think there also might have even been a Strawberries Record Store or Blockbuster Video anchoring either end. There's some context for you.

My destination that morning was a small non-descript audio store where I had dropped off a busted amplifier we used on DJ gigs. Pulling my Jeep Cherokee into a parking space in front of the shop, nothing seemed out of the ordinary. The only thing that did catch my attention was a lone figure in a hooded sweatshirt huddled near the door, looking like someone trying to hold off the wind in order to light a cigarette. As I opened the door to enter the shop, he followed closely behind. My attention was elsewhere, fixated on the two owners of the shop who were face down and tied up behind the counter, with several masked men holding guns to their heads, screaming for money and the combination to the safe. Just as my brain was processing what felt like a scene from a Martin Scorsese film, I felt the cold barrel of a shotgun press deep into the nape of my neck and heard the words nobody wants to hear, *"Keep walking and don't say a word or I'll blow your motherfucking head off!"* A sunny morning suddenly turned dark.

At that point I did the only prudent thing; I froze. Unable to move my extremities, I blinked several times to hopefully wake from this nightmare. But it was real and terrifying, very much like that out of body experience phenomena you hear about. With my mind's eye I saw a panorama of the shop with all of the principals, including me, in play. Weird, but not unusual. The feeling only lasted a few seconds before one of the bad guys shoved me by shotgun upstairs to a small loft area, forcing me to freeze in place face down on the floor. If I moved, well you can guess what was promised. Kneeling in the dark, I could hear them threatening the owners of the shop just yards away downstairs. *"Open the fuckin' safe or you're dead!"* Meanwhile, the one who had prodded me with the shotgun (my personal handler) relieved me of my wallet and keys before rejoining the gang. I was alone in this dusty unlit alcove thinking, "I'm going to die in a crummy little Stoneham audio repair shop at 10 o'clock in the morning. How absolutely pointless and anti-climactic!" Certainly not a Hollywood ending. Violent trauma is a fascinating full-body experience. I never felt as afraid in my life, but I was also oddly calm. No shaking, panting for breath or sweating. Just a vibrating numbness as though I was dosed with an adrenaline-laced hypodermic needle. And what they say about life flashing before you is true. Thirty-four years on high speed playback while the man that might kill me lurked nearby. My most profound memory was thinking that with Wendy seven months pregnant with our second child, he or she might never know their Dad. I tear up now writing about it.

I huddled there without a sense of real time for what might have been 15 or 20 minutes, thinking up jokes to stay focused (one about starring in a ghoulish remake of "Who shot J.R?"), when the front door opened and a male voice shouted, "Is anybody here? Everybody alright?" It was a customer stopping by to pick up an order. One of the sweetest sounds I can ever remember. By now the criminals had fled. None of us moved until that unsuspecting customer confirmed it.

Soon after the police arrived; three patrolmen and a plain clothes detective. I remember the detective telling us how lucky we all were because the perps were likely high on drugs, having tied us all up and positioned us execution-style. "I am surprised they didn't whack you," he said, at an obviously ill-attempt to make us feel better. Didn't work. "Yeah usually that's a bad sign for victims, often it ends with their murder." Apparently, the Stoneham Police Department wasn't high on sensitivity training back then. The detective asked for a description. I never saw their faces, but did remember the angry voice of a desperate man looking for cash.

Within minutes, more police arrived followed by reporters from the local press. The first person to arrive from Boston media was Charlie Austin, the veteran beat reporter for WBZTV 4. A few years later I would be working in the same building with him when I landed at WBZ Radio. When he arrived with a cameraman, I asked him quietly to help me out. "Charlie, I need you to do me a favor. Being on radio every day, I'm a bit of a public figure so if possible, can you not mention my name? Whoever did this might track me down and threaten my family." I had seen enough police procedurals to believe that the villain will stalk the witness. In reality, hoodlums usually forget about their victims. They just want to high-tail it out of there. Charlie complied. He did me a solid and I was forever appreciative. Austin went on to be inducted into the Massachusetts Broadcast Hall of Fame, retiring with the respect and admiration of his peers and community. He battled cancer and other illnesses for years, living a courageous and dignified life. He is greatly missed.

Although the bad guys had taken my car keys, they left the Jeep, how very thoughtful of them. I called my wife (spent at least two solid minutes assuring her I was fine, nothing to worry about, all was well, etc.) asking her to leave work (Wendy was a special needs high school teacher) to fetch a spare set of keys for the Jeep so I could get home. Our home town police were also notified and met us at the house, promising to patrol the neighborhood for the next several days, looking out for anyone suspicious. The following day, someone reported finding my wallet tossed on the side of the road, minus the $200 in cash I was planning to deposit that fateful day. I miss not one dime of that money. A small price to pay for dodging many bullets. The following day, Kenny and his brother Kurt (who is another of my long-standing friends) treated me to a celebratory lunch. We went to the Ritz-Carlton Boston, a grand dame hotel across from the Public Gardens, and drank champagne in honor of me living to tell the tale. It felt like a movie scene or something I had read in a novel. I was inches from losing my life and the shock had not even remotely taken hold.

Two months later, a day after my beautiful son Andrew was born, I was visited at home by an assistant district attorney from Suffolk County saying they had arrested suspects in the case, could I identify them? I reported honestly, that I never saw their faces and could only describe what one of them was wearing.

We could never figure out why they chose to rob a small mom-and-pop audio store that fixes and sells second-hand sound equipment. How much cash could have possibly been in that safe to make it worth the risk? I guess when you're a desperate criminal, desperate for drug money, a tiny suburban audio repair shop can seem like Fort Knox.

Yes, I survived that very scary day in October 1992. But what I didn't realize at the time was that the incident was a significant piece of a smoldering trauma fuse first lit three years prior. I didn't grasp the repercussions of not dealing with trauma that would lead to a disturbing breakdown. A much more frightening trip lay in wait.

In December of 1989 my wife, Wendy, was diagnosed with Hodgkin's Lymphoma, a cancer that originates from a specific type of white blood cells called lymphocytes. Symptoms may include fever, night sweats and weight loss, all of which Wendy developed. Outward signs are non-painful enlarged lymph nodes in the neck, under the arms or in the groin. We were concerned when she discovered a lump in her neck and the

132

process of diagnosis began. Hearing the word cancer associated with an otherwise healthy mid-thirties mom was devastating. But we lobbied hard to work with the best doctors available at Massachusetts General Hospital and they offered a treatment plan that could likely lead to remission. Of course with cancer there are never any guarantees. Following the recommended treatment course, she had her spleen removed (considered precautionary back then so cancer cells would be prevented from spreading to other organs via the spleen) and underwent radiation therapy five days a week for six long months. She was considered "cured" in 1991, with clean scans, but would need to go regularly for checkups. For anyone who has dealt with cancer (sadly most of us), the agony is in the wait for test results, coping with challenging treatments, and dealing with countless emotional stressors.

Our daughter Lindsay was born in 1987, two years prior to Wendy's diagnosis. Treatments and recuperation meant we needed to wait for some time to try for another child. Wendy did get pregnant in 1991 with the pregnancy sadly resulting in a miscarriage. Wendy was stoic and thoughtful that it wasn't meant to be and we could try again. Happily, our son Andrew was conceived in early 1992 (seven months before my encounter at the audio store). What I didn't know at the time (and honestly how could I?) was that the combination of these life altering events—my wife's cancer, the birth of children, the holdup—plus working far too many hours during the week and on the road nearly every weekend, was causing my mental state to simmer on its way to a full-on boil. And in the summer of 1995, the lid finally blew.

On a beautiful Sunday morning in June of 1995, after a long stretch of non-stop work, I had the feeling that something was off. The day before, after a sore throat I had for a few days worsened, I stopped by the local Health-Stop drive-in clinic and was prescribed an antibiotic, hoping it would quell the pain and lessen any infection. A bum throat with all that I had to do behind the mic back then was not fun. Along with poor sleep habits, I was eating on the go and was overdoing black coffee, consuming four to five cups a day. That Sunday morning things seemed out of focus. I couldn't concentrate on much without feeling uncomfortable and edgy. Even playing with the kids or eating breakfast seemed like a struggle. Here was a feeling I had never experienced before, an overriding anxiety, coupled with a lack of interest, a listless feeling that would settle in for days. I attributed it to the infection I had been fighting and certainly thought it would pass. Mind you, I've always been blessed with excellent health. I'm thin, with low blood pressure, no pre-existing conditions, a high level of stamina—or so I thought. But here I was grumpy and jumpy with a racing mind, thinking I was nearing the end of my years, running out of time, irrational, upsetting thoughts that I couldn't turn off. Finally, after some prodding from Wendy, I made an appointment to see my doctor. What he told me after a brief exam shocked me. My doctor of 25 years said I displayed all the signs of clinical depression. I forced a chuckle as I thought how could I, the happiest guy in every crowd, be depressed? I have a great career, a loving wife and kids. Yes, I work a lot, but so do many people. He prescribed Zoloft, an antidepressant to ease the symptoms. But he said it would be best to couple the medication with talk therapy. Again, I was dubious. Talk therapy? In other words, see a shrink? That would be an admission of what, mental illness? I, like so many others, thought of depression as a character flaw, not the actual illness that it is. This wasn't depression. It had to be symptoms of burnout due to overwork. Still, I listened to the doctor whom I had trusted for decades and went off to fill the prescription.

What we know about anti-depressant medication then and now is that for some people it offers salvation, saving them from a lifetime of despair, fatigue, lethargy and pain. For others, the medications fail to work or it might take months or years of weaning off one to try another until relief arrives. With depression, there is a lag time of anywhere from two to 10 weeks before serotonin focused meds "kick in." There is hell in waiting. You count the days, hours and minutes hoping the drug might work. No guarantee. In a culture where instant pain relief is what we have all come to expect, the wait for any sign of improvement is like serving hard time. And not one of those country club white collar prisons. No, more like the Bastille or Alcatraz. It sucks.

As I said, my caring doctor recommended I "speak with someone about my feelings." I consider myself open-minded, but the idea of opening up to a psychiatrist, psychologist or social worker was not in my comfort zone. At the time, I didn't know the difference among the three. Happy to say I am now educated and truly open-minded when it comes to mental health. I told the doctor I had nothing to talk about. The problem was in my body not my head, "So can we just get to work fixing me?" I figured the scary thoughts and sensations would abate once my physical condition got straightened out. I had no idea what was in store. Cocky describes my attitude, imagining what lay ahead. I was climbing defenseless into the ring with Mike Tyson. That's how hard depression can punch.

So, my journey as a newly diagnosed depression sufferer began. I did a ton of research wanting to know more, and why me. For several months I suffered alone, with only Wendy and my doctor knowing the diagnosis. It would end up taking years to uncover the root psychological causes of the illness, but I knew this much; this was by far the strongest, most relentless challenge I was to ever face. As strong-willed and disciplined as I am, I couldn't thwart the pain, fear and sadness that would wash over me, always at inappropriate times. Any stigma I harbored about mental illness went away once I joined the not so-exclusive depression club. I poured over books on the subject in my spare time, seeking understanding and hope. Many books, such as *Darkness Visible*, a depression memoir by writer William Styron and *Care for the Soul*, by religion scholar and therapist Thomas Moore (whom I adore and would later interview on more than one occasion) sustained me somewhat through the pain. And out of darkness has come light. I've looked at all I have gained by dropping to the bottom of my own personal elevator shaft, only to rebuild myself on the climb back up. But there's no denying that over the course of many years, I was miserable. Depression can often recur, striking on its own schedule. I felt worse on beautiful summer days and often skipped on further downward while on vacation. The low hum of anxiety was often present, causing me to lose focus at meetings, parties, work and home life. The 'black dog' as Winston Churchill referred to depression, plays by its own cruel rules.

You're in the octagon with the world's toughest MMA fighter. Your job is to hang in there, learn how the healing arc works and bask in gratitude when that healing starts to happen.

Medically, my depression was classified as moderate. I was able to function well enough to get through the workday, fulfill nearly all of my obligations and "fake it" with most people including my children who were still pretty young at the time. I didn't want the kids to see their Dad in pain or exhibiting weakness, particularly in light of their Mom's struggles with cancer. Turns out my training as a young actor served me well, especially at the radio station. No one seemed to know what I was going through. I would buck up and push through my morning show with the usual upbeat demeanor. But the extra effort it took to perform at that level tuckered me out. Not to mention those hours, with me rising by 3:00am daily. Sleep was spotty at best. Occasionally while on the air alone in the studio, I'd shut the mic after introducing a song, and put my head down for an unprovoked cry. The release of tears always left me feeling better, the body's way of washing away pain. Finding a time and a place for a private sob became an activity of mine.

Kenny knew about the depression as it unfolded, as did Wendy. Confiding in those closest was a key to my recovery. I eventually shared the news with my parents; not feeling right hiding it from them. My mother, who would have made a darned good private eye, suspected something was up. Tough to fool a pro like her. My parents were actually more understanding than I ever thought they would be, which was an emotional relief.

But on radio and in public, it was "put on a happy face" and business as usual. Good old fun-loving Jordan Rich, the man with a humorous line for any occasion, who brings smiles to his listeners daily. But as Smokey Robinson once sang, "Though

I'm laughing long and hearty, deep inside I'm blue." How true. You can analogize depression coupled with anxiety like this. It is like you're in a foreign country and trying to communicate but nobody speaks your language or seems to care. They're all happy and having fun, while you're sad and a mess. It is frustrating and maddening. Until you realize that everyone is carrying pain around with them. It's that human condition we hear so much about. And I am ever so human.

Did I ever feel my career was threatened by it? Depression rocked me hard and my self-esteem and self-confidence took big hits. I would sit in my idling car before dawn in the station's parking lot and say to myself, "I'm not sure I should go inside. What if I break down on the air?" I would then suck it up and walk into the studio, my comfort zone, and the fear lessened. Having years of experience in the business helped. My performer instincts were taxed but prevailed. Still, it was frightening.

Besides being on-air, I had speaking engagements and master of ceremony assignments that were challenging. There was anxiety of appearing weak or flustered. Granted, no one ever noticed as far as I could tell, but the illness plays with your head and rattles your self-confidence.

One day in the summer of 1995 during the early rough days of the depression, I was assigned to host an event at Boston's City Hall Plaza in front of several thousand adults and children. On stage with me was the honorable mayor of Boston at the time, Tom Menino. "The guest of honor" and the reason for the throngs of fans was an appearance by Barney the Purple Dinosaur. There wasn't a cloud in the sky on this sunny morning. My kids were with me, by the side of the stage with their Mom, in front of thousands of screaming Barney fans. I wanted to jump off the stage to hide just about anywhere. Fortunately, my experience as an entertainer got me through it. The gig went off smoothly. We had pictures taken with the purple reptile and my smile was beaming as I somehow held it together. Photos can lie. The Mayor, the press, the crowds. But I believe it was Lindsay and Andrew I was most concerned about letting down.

The following week, on the evening of July 4th, I took Lindsay to see the new *Batman* movie at the Framingham Showcase Cinemas. The theatre was packed with excited fans. Normally,

I would have loved a film like that. Instead I was fidgety and anxious, doing all I could to pretend I was okay in front of my daughter. I got up at one point and told her to sit tight as Dad just has to use the restroom and will be right back. I went into the bathroom, sat in a stall, locked the door and broke down in tears for several minutes.

Over the next several years I'd rebound and feel good again, only to have my old friend, "the creep" as I dubbed it, return; sometimes milder, at others more intense. I test drove more than my share of therapists and psychologists, trying different approaches. None seemed to take hold and work long term. The therapists all seemed to offer the same pathway to healing—to "feel" the pain and not hide from emotions. That makes sense academically. Dealing with feelings is a lot easier though when not weighed down by the physical symptoms of depression and anxiety. It wasn't until several years later that I enlisted the help of a top flight psychiatrist who was able to properly regulate my medication needs. With the correct medication and dosage, I was able to do the kind of talk therapy that bore fruit, allowing me to grow into a more well-balanced person.

Life continued to present challenges for our family. In 2002, Wendy had a recurrence of cancer cells in her thyroid and the decision was made to undergo chemotherapy. Losing her hair, incurring weakness and making many runs to Boston for treatments was tiring for both of us, but she again showed remarkable resilience, and after six months was in the clear. The cancer was gone. We were ecstatic at the news and began a new chapter raising the family, enjoying more time off, appreciating the people in our lives. But cancer, like its horrid cousin depression, lurks in the shadows, returning to cause pain. In 2011, we received some very tough news after Wendy struggled with a nagging cough; she was diagnosed with Mesothelioma, a deadly form of cancer that erupts in the thin layer of tissue that covers most of the lungs. Many cases of Mesothelioma are attributed to working in factories laden with asbestos. Wendy never worked in such a place. Sadly, the cause of her disease was traced back to the intense radiation therapy that she received in 1989, the first time she had cancer. What cured her then, was about to take her from us now. She was philosophical about it, often saying in her final days that she got twenty good years of life thanks to that earlier therapy. I was demoralized when following last ditch but hopeful clinical trials, we were told there was nothing more that could be done. She passed away peacefully while in hospice care in 2013, leaving a daughter three months from her wedding date and a son in his first year of college. She also left me, the upbeat husband, father and radio personality. Now a man alone experiencing a new form of grief.

I was stressed and saddened throughout the final cancer journey. But luckily, I did not experience the physical torment of depression at that time. I'm grateful that by then I had beaten it back. Now the sadness was authentic and justifiable.

Let's rewind just a bit to tell you of a decision I made a few years prior that helped me to heal. I was working at Boston's talk and news station WBZ, taking late-night calls from all around the country *("Dan in Ohio, go ahead, you're on the air.")*. More on my time as a late-night host in the next chapter, but this was the radio gig I was made for. Over time we developed the Jordan Rich Show into a popular spot on the dial for warm conversation, a potpourri of interviews with leading writers, historians, actors and personalities. And I developed a close kinship with the audience.

One night, with no guests scheduled, an epiphany came over me. I decided it was time to share my "secret" with the audience. I thought, God, why am I hiding this? They knew me so well; I've been here hosting for over 10 years. We had shared quite a bit. They knew about my kids, about Wendy's illnesses, my love of film, food, comedy, and my off-air pursuits. I began raising money for the station's charity Boston Children's Hospital and so many of the audience were generous, helping me raise hundreds of thousands of dollars. I felt safe that night relating my story of depression; I didn't want to fake it in the public anymore and thought maybe I could help others by letting them know they weren't alone in their struggle. Knowing I was not alone certainly helped me. So I did it. It was midnight when we started the broadcast that beamed to 38 states and much of Canada. I opened the show saying I needed to be very honest about something that had been going on in my life for a long time. I wanted to unburden myself, and by doing so help others at the same time. It was emotional for me. My monologue laid out the story and there were times I did tear up. It caught everyone, including the producer on the other side of the glass by surprise. As soon as my heart to heart talk ended, we took the commercial break and promised to take a few calls.

It ended up being way more than a few. Folks from all over the country called in talking about themselves or loved ones who had suffered with depression, some who got better, others who did not. Doctors and mental health nurses called in as they headed into or back from their late shifts. It opened up a deeply emotional stream of conversation, empathy and understanding for me and many listeners. I think of it as a personal and professional highlight, the chance to be real, to provide inspiration to many, and to build back my confidence.

As I said, it wasn't until I began working with the right doctor in 2010, that I was able to take back my life fully. A highly-respected psychiatrist at Massachusetts General Hospital was recommended by a friend whom I had worked with in radio and whose husband knew the doctor personally. It turns out he was also a depression sufferer. By 2010, after 15 years wading through waves of depression and anxiety it was time to try a new approach, one more medically mainstream. What made my new doctor stand out was her keen understanding of psychopharmacology, as well as her empathy and wisdom. In working together, we were able to explore several variants – physical, mental, emotional – at the same time. She has been a godsend. I still check in with her and maintain a regimen of solid sleep, exercise, diet, meditation and more to stay well.

After the on-air confessions, I felt relieved. The days of covering up and "acting" had ended. Depression and other mental health conditions are not character flaws, they are illnesses. The stigma still exists, but as the years go by people are coming around to the idea that we're all human, experiencing a range of highs and lows, dealing with stress as best we can. Some of us need a helping hand to get by.

Along with the medication adjustments and therapy, I still felt the need to ease up on my schedule. I had been hosting Friday and Saturday overnights, and then doing a Sunday late evening shift. The Monday after the "big reveal" weekend, I went to see Peter Casey, WBZ's Program Director at the time, and told him about my desire to cut back on the Sunday show. I shared with him about my depression over the years. He completely understood and was supportive in every way. I retained the two overnight shows and never did Peter or anyone on the staff treat me any differently. I'm grateful.

A lot of wonderful people are living with the conditions I described and many are still hiding as I did. Often, they self medicate with drugs and alcohol to escape the incessant pain. Depression drives you nuts because you think you're going crazy and that it's your fault. My opinion is that it's not. You're human. Connect with others who can and will help you. And when you heal as I have, the renewed balance and vigor will promote gratitude. That's a very good thing.

CHAPTER SEVEN
WBZ: Working On Those Night Moves

"Hi, Jordan. This is Bill Flaherty over at WBZ. Do you remember me?"

Perhaps next to having Publishers Clearing House ringing my bell, armed with balloons and an oversized check, this call from Bill Flaherty at WBZ-AM1030 Radio, was akin to the Red Sox telling me to hop on the bus in Pawtucket and get my butt up to Boston. This was WBZ, the big leagues, blasting out a 50,000-watt signal that reached 38 states.

Before continuing, let me explain my euphoria, in the context of Boston radio history.

WBZ Radio went on the air September 19, 1921, as one of the first licensed commercial radio stations in America. The honor of being the first goes to KDKA in Pittsburgh. Our radio station, owned by Westinghouse, originally operated out of two locations; Boston and Springfield. Eventually studios were combined at a downtown Boston hotel. As one of the oldest and most powerful radio stations in the area, WBZ became a popular spot at 1030 on the AM dial. It made news on April 28, 1932 when a thought-to-be tame circus lion was brought to the studio, only to have it run amok, injuring seven employees and damaging much of the equipment. In September of 1938, WBZ broadcast its first hurricane report. There is no truth to the rumor that Shelby Scott, a local TV reporter famous in New England for reporting live in the midst of storms, provided coverage from a Scituate seawall. Shelby would have just been learning her ABC's at that time.

The 1940s introduced morning man Carl DeSuze to New England, the 1950s brought us everyone's favorite meteorologist Don Kent and popular DJ Dave Maynard. We can thank the 1960s for Bruce Bradley, Dick Summer, Gary LaPierre, Larry Glick, Gil Santos and the birth of sports talk radio with "Calling All Sports," hosted by the erudite Guy Mainella, in July 1969. Lovell Dyett and Bob Raleigh appeared on the scene in the 1970s, followed by David Brudnoy in the 1980s. These names read like a "Who's Who" in broadcasting. Today they are considered Boston radio legends. I was soon to be working in the very same studio that introduced them. Pinch me!

But back to Bill Flaherty and his call in September 1996. I was in my office at Chart Productions, nine months since being fired from WSSH. And in *radio years*, nine months is like nine years! There was reason to worry. Was it pretty much over for me in Boston radio? Would I have to start all over again in a smaller market, trying to scratch my way back slowly? Would it be worth it?

Out of the blue comes that phone call from WBZ. Of course I remembered Bill; he would occasionally call me for an easy favor when I was at WSSH early mornings. Bill was a news producer at the time and with WBZ having switched to an all-news and talk format, he didn't have access to music. The record library was sent packing and this was well before online downloads. If there was a major concert coming to town, WBZ would want to do a short feature with the star's music needed to complete the segment. I would grab a song from the WSSH library and make a reel-to-reel dub, then leave it at the front desk for Bill to fetch. Simple, and all told I might have done it three times over the years. Bill said that he never forgot what I did for him. A little favor can go a long way.

He asked if I was interested in filling in for one night for one of my mentors, Norm Nathan. Working with Norm at WRKO was exhilarating. I learned much from him about humor, pacing and timing, not to mention how radio can indeed become "theatre of the mind." I also got to appreciate more about classic jazz, one of Norm's passions. 'The Old Sport' meant the world to me and the idea of filling in for him, even for just one night, was exciting.

Norm's wife, former newspaper gossip columnist Norma Nathan, had passed away a few years earlier, leaving him alone on his little suburban farm, with the radio show the thing, I believe, that kept him going. Now getting on in years, Norm's two daughters were on him to take a well-deserved vacation, having recently celebrated his 50th anniversary on Boston radio. The girls bought him an all-expense paid cruise to the Caribbean, which he grudgingly accepted. It meant him taking one weekend off from WBZ. Bill Flaherty barely finished his question about my availability when I said I'd be flattered, honored and excited for the opportunity. I'm sure I sounded breathless. My debut on the biggest, most prestigious station in Boston would happen in days.

I remember the Saturday of the show vividly. I had DJ'ed a party that afternoon and had more than my usual share of yelling to do (corralling dozens of 13-year olds at a raucous bar mitzvah) and ended up losing most of my voice by the end of the day. Laryngitis rarely struck, but this was a doozy. Why then? Not to be defeated, I took action, pouring honey into endless cups of tea while chain-sucking lozenges. By the time I arrived at WBZ on Soldiers Field Road to meet the producer who would show me the ropes, I had barely a whisper left. At 12:05 when the music rolled, I summoned all of the intestinal fortitude and phlegm I could muster and with pure adrenaline began to live a dream. The voice held up through the night, in the same studio that Norm and Dave Maynard, David Brudnoy and Gary LaPierre broadcast from. A few yards down the hall were the studios for WBZ-TV Channel 4, where as a 5-year old I was part of the posse on *Rex Trailer's Boomtown Show*, one of the most popular local TV kid shows. Rex, another boyhood hero, would end up being a friend. He was often a guest on my show and over the years we joined forces on many audio projects.

Back to the debut. Upon arriving (clearing my throat endlessly) I was introduced to the workings of the on-air studio.

I would not be running the controls, save for my mic switch and telephone board. The producer from behind the soundproof glass would answer and prep the callers, placing them in queue. The names would then appear on my screen. The all important number (like my social security number I could never forget it AND it's still in service today) was 617-254-1030. I had practiced the call letters and that fabled number hundreds of times in the car on my way to and from gigs. There was no topic or agenda that night. It was what we refer to as an "open lines" program. Let me add here, that no one in programming ever directed me to foster a particular point of view or choice of guests or subjects. More on that later.

My game plan that night was pretty straight-forward. I would introduce myself to the large nationwide audience with a simple question, "What are you doing up this late?" Nothing controversial and hopefully somewhat interesting. The first name on the call screen posted by the producer was "Virginia." I was pumped to take my first call ever on WBZ, something I had fantasized about. Clearing my throat again (I did make use of the cough button religiously), I flipped the switch opening line one and said warmly "Hello Virginia!" The voice on the other end said, "This is Sarah." I said, "Oh, sorry about that. I'm new here and it says Virginia on the screen." She said, 'No, I'm Sarah, and I'm *calling* from Virginia." That's when the power of the WBZ signal hit me, at that moment my voice was travelling well beyond Route 128 and the confines of Boston to many parts of our vast country. I was part of a select few broadcasting on a 50,000-WATT clear channel signal with no night time restrictions. Somewhere out there, a young kid would be listening under the covers as I once did.

I did the show that night until 5:00am and by all accounts it went well. Norm returned the following week. I called to thank him for recommending me to fill-in for him. He told me he had nothing to do with it, but was glad someone suggested me for it. We talked for a while with me assuring Norm I'd be listening when he returned on Saturday. He replied in typical "Uncle Norm" fashion, "Well, Little Buster (his nickname for me when we worked together) that will be just so darned swell!" It was only a month later when sadly, Norm passed away. He had been in failing health for a while and died peacefully in his sleep. The audience was heartbroken as were all who knew and worked with him. I remember attending his funeral along with hundreds of friends and listeners. The service featured a live performance by a talented husband and wife duo, Mike Palter and Lynn Jackson whom I adore. They performed two of Norm's favorite songs in a gorgeous medley; "The Colors of My Life," from the Broadway show *Barnum*, and "Sing a Rainbow," composed by Arthur Hamilton for the film *Pete Kelly's Blues*.

These are two soulful songs that invoke feelings of hope, comfort and imagination. The lyrics from "The Colors of my Life," are especially lovely, promoting the idea that those colors will leave a shining light to guide us along our way.

The service featured an outpouring of love for a radio performer who for 50 years delivered so much to listeners. What a legacy.

Radio always goes on. There has to be someone on-air to ensure continuity. Like the U.S. Post Office, we're dedicated to being there for you. The WBZ Program Director, Peter Casey, asked me and others to fill in after Norm died until they could come up with a permanent replacement. For the next several weeks, I alternated with longtime WBZ veteran Dave Maynard on the midnight to 6:00am Saturday and Sunday shifts. Much of the time was spent remembering Norm, celebrating his humor and all that he meant to WBZ and Boston. Listeners from across the country and Canada were calling in steadily to pay their respects.

So, I reported for duty as an outside vendor for over a month. Finally, by the end of December, Peter called me in and said, "You know, we were all saddened by Norm's passing, but if anyone's going to take over this shift and do the kind of show that Norm did, I think it should be you. Would you consider it?"

I was honored, excited and more than a bit anxious of what lay ahead. I humbly accepted. During my time filling in I felt a developing connection with the audience, relying on so much of what Norm taught me about self-deprecation and treating listeners with kindness and respect. One has to know one's listeners to form a lasting bond.

One of the things I did early on was approach Norm's daughters with the idea of producing a "best of" cassette featuring some of his classic radio bits, his theme song (Count Basie's "Midnight Blue,") and a testimonial or two from some special friends. Why the idea for such a tribute? Well, on a nightly basis callers were requesting we play his old routines ("The Swap Shop," Norm checking his celebrity answering machine, hysterical commercials he was well known for, etc.).

People were hungry for their favorite Norm moments, they didn't want to say goodbye.

Kenny Carberry and I formulated the idea. We got permission from Peter Casey, and after meeting with Norm's daughters Sonja and Sara, we produced a "Best of Norm Nathan" cassette (later a CD) with all proceeds going to charity. It took a few months to gather material, write the intro which I voiced, interview some of Norm's friends and fans such as standup comic Steven Wright, and develop the artwork. With the help of Kenny, we produced it, made hundreds of copies and I promoted it on the air. We sold hundreds, with the money raised funding a jazz scholarship in perpetuity in Norm's name at Berkeley College of Music. It was an appropriate passing of the torch. He deserved to be honored and remembered. It was a labor of love that I look back on proudly as one of our best.

As the months rolled on, I put my own stamp on the program and it even had a name that was easy for me to remember—The Jordan Rich Show! Again, the station pretty much gave me free reign. I decided early on that I didn't want to do an issues-oriented hard line talk show. I don't like fighting with people, confrontation is not my thing, never will be. Political divides were not as harsh as they are today, but things were starting to get a bit ugly with the Clinton-era scandals. So, I went with what brought me here, interviewing guests from all walks of life—authors, artists, historians, humorists and more. My intent was and has always been to satisfy my curiosity while entertaining and educating. It's a mistake many broadcasters make, believing that because they think something is fascinating, that all listeners will agree. To get people to listen, the broadcaster must learn to listen.

I soon developed specialty theme nights. Every few months I'd present a movie night with a group of us talking about favorite films, actors, genres. As much fun as it was, the folks I had with me knew their stuff. People such as former Boston TV reporter Garry Armstrong. Garry loved classic films, having interviewed many stars from Hollywood's golden age. Another serious movie buff is a dear friend named Gary King. His family (Dad and several brothers) was in the special effects business making movie magic for decades and Gary himself worked on such classics as *Young Frankenstein* and *The Towering Inferno*. He had moved to southern New England after retiring from the movie industry and would regale us with stories. There were other themed shows including TV nights, restaurant nights (call in to recommend a favorite diner or 5-star restaurant), trivia nights of all varieties, and the most popular one of all, the "Jordan Rich Show Book Night." A simple concept, designed to make life a bit easier for me in the wee small hours when calls were hard to come by. I'd invite people to call in with book recommendations, new and old, fiction and non-fiction, by local authors as well as nationally renowned authors. It was a hit from the very first show with all phone lines fully lit. In the early days pre-widespread Internet, I would comprise the list of recommended titles and authors and make it available to those who wrote or called in for a copy. That meant a lot of work composing and printing up the list (trying to get titles and author's name spelled right before Google was challenging), then burning the pre-midnight oil and more than a few toner cartridges making copies on the newsroom Xerox. Then, mailing them out, by hand, no doubt hundreds over the years. In fact, my franking privileges might have rivaled that of any congressional office. I reckon between the lists, correspondence and prizes to listeners (tickets, books, T-shirts, pens, key chains and related "merch,"), the station's postage budget due to me was exceedingly high. I'm grateful to the station to have had the chance to connect with so many folks that way.

There were many memorable events. On August 31, 1997, I had guests booked only to abruptly cancel them as the news came across that Princess Diana of Britain had died in a car crash in Paris at approximately 11:45pm (EST), 15 minutes before airtime. With no yardstick to gauge the impact of such an event, I went with my gut, opening the lines so people could vent upon hearing the tragic news. The board lit up and calls came in all night from people across the country, expressing sadness, anger and confusion. None of us knew Diana personally, but most were shaken by her sudden, senseless death. It became a cathartic radio experience with many calling in to relate personal losses. I received positive mail for months for the way we handled things that night. Another tragedy that happened on a weekend involved the death of John F. Kennedy, Jr. in a plane crash off Martha's Vineyard. There was a similar reaction of disbelief, this time for someone much closer to home, a member of the Kennedy family. I developed a keener sense of empathy and found myself maturing as a listener during such moments. When the economic collapse of 2008 occurred, I took calls from people who were depressed about

161

losing their savings, their jobs, their futures. My role became that of comforter. I had no grand answers, but was a familiar voice on radio offering to listen and offer a message of hope. The most jarring event of course involved the terror attacks on 9-11. Anger, fear, and uncertainty were all magnified during the crisis. We tried our best both on the news and talk radio sides to present the truth, to dismiss rumor and false leads, to be as responsible with factual, helpful information as possible. Sadly, much of media today have chosen sensationalism and conjecture over truth. We were far from perfect but felt an obligation to at least try to present different sides of a story, to allow for differing points of view.

Some interesting observations about being up late and working third shift. First off, the stress wreaks havoc on one's body and biological clock. That's a given. But there are also plusses—

less traffic congestion, cleaner air and a quieter overall environment. Most of us look forward to relaxing, letting our guard down when darkness falls. The night can have a soothing effect. It certainly did on me. I became more relaxed as an announcer, much more comfortable speaking honestly after midnight. My radio persona over the years was of a positive, funny, and caring guy. But I developed a more intimate connection with the late-night audience.

Like a late-night minister, I provided free counseling sessions for listeners. So much of the job was listening. People wanted to be heard. Others who would never think of calling, would relate to or be entertained by the stories the callers shared. Most of the time it was light and fun chatting with people about the worst date they ever had or their run-ins with celebrities. Senior citizens would call in to tell me about their grandchildren or reminisce about the "good old days." Of course, news issues of the day, pop culture, sports, politics, etc., were all topics on the table.

On a few occasions, the personal conversations took on a more somber, serious tone. One involved a guy named Joe. Joe was the only caller in my many years on air who spoke openly of committing suicide. I took the call on a Saturday morning at 4:06am. His voice was weak as he choked back tears about losing his job, and not being allowed to see his only daughter following a bitter divorce. Joe was seriously depressed and appeared to have lost his will to go on.

I kept him on the line and recommended he speak to someone professionally or at least contact the Samaritans, whose number I kept on hand (I also never did a talk show without a copy of the U.S. Constitution and at least one Almanac, even after Google came along). We talked for nearly a half hour. As we ended he vowed to seek help, I said goodbye, wished him God's blessing and good luck. I then reflected on what the audience and I had heard, how Joe's hurt was palpable and many would likely relate. Following a commercial break, several called in to offer their support, urging Joe to hang in there, to get help. That included a psychiatric nurse who heard the conversation driving home from her shift. She insisted to Joe (we assumed he was still listening, certainly hoped so) that "I want you to know we can help you, and there is a place to turn." That sweet nurse left her number and details about the facility at which she worked. Joe was asked to leave his address with the producer. I sent Joe a long letter in which I shared my personal struggles with depression, as well as information supplied by that nurse. I tried to check up on him the next day but found it difficult to reach him by phone or email. The story, however, has a satisfying ending.

Several months passed. I was prepping to go on-air at midnight, and the last caller on the program preceding me, hosted by a wonderful friend and local broadcast legend Lovell Dyett, was named Joe. He began telling his story to Lovell about a night eight months ago when he called WBZ very late, despondent with no one to talk too, save the gentleman on the radio. He recounted, that had he not had that chance to talk with somebody, he might have ended his life that night. Since then, after hitting bottom, he got the help he needed and turned his life around, eventually getting back on his feet with a new job. He also resolved some differences with his ex-wife and was allowed to be in his daughter's life once again. I knew from his voice it was the same guy, a guy named Joe, whom I met on-air many months earlier. Hearing the happy ending story from Joe ranks as one of my most gratifying moments. As a Jew, I subscribe to the concept of *Tikkun Alom,* translated to mean any activity that improves the world brings it closer to the harmonious state for which it was created, even if it means helping one person at a time. Joe reinforced the importance of *Tikkun Alom* for me.

The show was an integral part of my life. I still worked weekdays at Chart Productions and would record some interviews there for airing on the weekends. During the week I would also schedule show guests and handle bookings. I also became a voracious reader, consuming three to five books per week to prep for the show. Scanning and speed-reading tricks came in handy. Few turned down an invitation to appear on the show. The reach of WBZ was well-known. With twelve hours of open air time, I made it a point to pack it full of compelling content. Most shows would feature four to six segments—interviews, celebrity guests, open lines, contests, readings, etc.

Many guests do stand out. Stan Lee, the creator of "Spider Man" and dozens of Marvel heroes was a guest of mine twice. I loved Stan as did his fans that crowded on to the phone lines to talk with him. Stan sent me not one but two handwritten thankyou notes on official "Spider Man" stationary. They adorn my office wall to this day. We had Carl Reiner, who spent two glorious hours talking about Mel Brooks, the Dick Van Dyke Show and everything showbiz. Liza Minnelli was delightful, decidedly down to earth and gracious. As was Lily Tomlin, George Carlin and Tony Bennett. I had the distinct honor of being "insulted" by Don Rickles one night. I stood in the shadow of Hulk Hogan, met and interviewed Moses himself, Charlton Heston, as well as one of the greatest sci-fi writers

166

ever, Ray Bradbury, and Hollywood icon, Kirk Douglas. There were many more non-celebrities, people from all walks of life who joined the late-night family. There is a more extensive list of guests in the back of this book. I'm amazed at how many I connected with over two decades!

I remember an emotionally-charged interview with an elderly writer named Ben Jacobs. In 1941, Berek Jakubowicz, as he was known then, was deported from his Polish village and became a Jewish prisoner of the Nazis until the end of the war. His rudimentary skills as a dentist saved his life. He wrote the memoir, *The Dentist of Auschwitz.* Over the course of my career I've interviewed well over a thousand authors (As mentioned, I read a ton and still do. Love it!). Other guests included philosophers, poets, inventors, historians and the occasional oddball. I had them all—magicians, hypnotists, psychics, animal trainers, improv troupes. And let's not forget music. So many nights were spent talking with professional musicians from all aspects of the business. We could only play short excerpts of their music due to licensing restrictions, but sharing conversations with jazz, classical, rock, Broadway and American Songbook stars was a joy and listeners loved it.

Another longstanding joke was that I featured more music on this AM talk show than was heard on most FM stations!

One regular guest was pianist Jeffrey Moore, who was a fixture as the lounge pianist at the Four Seasons Hotel in Boston. Jeffrey is a music machine, an incredible pianist who can play by ear over 4,000 American standards. I met him one night at the hotel. We got to talking between sets and I invited him on the show. He came, lugging a full-size electric keyboard that sounded very much like a baby grand. And it became request hour with callers asking for songs with special meaning. Jeffrey would play anything requested and in a style that was creative and elegant. We did dozens of shows over the years. He now lives out west in a beautiful desert home with his perfectly tuned grand piano!

The goal was to offer a late-night variety show where new topics and guests were coming right up. I felt an obligation to keep things fresh for the audience. We never expected anyone to be glued to the radio for five straight hours, although there were a few diehards who were. But with folks drifting in and out at different times, we kept up a steady stream of content with plenty of variety.

As fine a time as I was having at WBZ, lurking occasionally outside the studio door was my old unwanted companion, depression. It would come on gradually, starting out with a flashing recollection, building to a steady uncomfortable malaise before it would ebb and sneak off again into the shadows. During these episodes, that might last for weeks or months, the place where I felt most at ease was on-air. Being focused on delivering a quality show, on an artistic level, offered the perfect temporary respite from pain. And the nights, as mentioned, were always calmer, anxiety took a back seat to the performance. For many of us, meditative practice comes easier at night. Broadcasting is my art and meditation.

During my hosting days, the WBZ sales and promotion teams often asked me to serve as the station spokesperson. I loved doing commercials and promos, and represented WBZ in the community. Through Chart Productions, Kenny and I had worked with the Boston Symphony and the Boston Pops handling their radio marketing. We still work with them today, a relationship that has spanned three decades. So, I was a logical choice to be named radio host of the *Boston Pops Fireworks Spectacular* for which WBZ radio had exclusive rights. I ended up anchoring the event for 12 years, live from the Esplanade along the Charles River. Not only did I meet and interview famous guests of the Pops, such as Neil Diamond, Arlo Guthrie and The Beach Boys, but the crew and I had the best seats in America for the fireworks spectacular!

Being associated with a station as prestigious as WBZ opened many doors. I became a speaker on the circuit and emcee at numerous charity functions, auctions, and awards ceremonies. Once the Internet *did* become the thing, I created a web site and social media standing that boosted my presence, leading to more bookings. Email enabled all of us to connect instantly with listeners, community groups, and artists. My radio footprint expanded greatly with more contacts, guests, national reach and exposure.

With a long, trusted connection with our listeners, I felt comfortable sharing certain personal things with them. I had occasionally talked about Wendy's cancer, the ups and downs of remission and recurrence. As mentioned in a prior chapter, in 2011 she had a relapse of the cancer and after a year and half long final battle succumbed to the disease. It was grueling on all of us, particularly hard for the kids. After her passing, I was off the air for three weeks, dealing with the grief, doing all of the things expected of a mourner, such as offering comfort to my children, handling financial and legal paperwork, making all necessary arrangements. I decided when I came back to the airwaves not to ignore what had happened. People knew why I was out, I wanted them to hear the story from me, to share and move on. I chose to spend the first hour back telling the story, talking about our family's loss. I owed listeners that much. I instructed the producer not to take any phone calls for the hour. My intension was to honor Wendy, to reflect on the loss, and finally move on with the show. There was no script for this monologue, just a few notes scribbled on a 3x5 card.

I talked about the progression of the illness, the sense of peace when it was over, the vagueness of loss. I spoke of the incredible efforts of the doctors and nurses who tried their very best, how our family was coping, why sharing with the audience felt like the right thing to do. Halfway through the hour, with eyes misty, I noticed one lone phone line blinking on hold for many minutes. I ignored it. During a commercial break the producer spoke to me over the intercom. "JR, you really ought to consider taking this call." I responded, "Thanks, but I told them I don't want to take any calls this hour. It's better if I just move through what I have to say uninterrupted, hard enough as it is." The intercom opened again and the producer stressed, "No, you *really* need to take this call." I trusted my colleague, felt that way about so many who worked with me over the years, so with about 10 minutes left to go in the hour I pressed the button to place the caller on the air. I'm so very glad I did take the call.

"Hello, I don't know what you want to add or who you are, but I'm told to take this call, so welcome you're on WBZ…"

The caller turned out to be one of Wendy's nurses who attended her nine months earlier when she had major surgery to remove a cancerous lung in an effort to save her. This beautiful sweet nurse from Massachusetts General Hospital told us she normally didn't listen at this time but her shift was recently changed and here she was. She called (and I feel the swell of emotion as I recall this) simply to say how wonderful it was to take care of my late wife, how Wendy was committed to making it and talked only about our family while in recovery. The call from the nurse was touching, a blessing of kindness and compassion. I wanted to reach through the phone line to hug her. As we ended our conversation, both of us welling up a bit, the hour came to a close and I announced the goal was to

172

move on in a new direction following the news. Well, that didn't happen. For the next four hours the calls never stopped. All wanted to express condolences. But also, to talk about their personal losses, how we measure the value of our loved ones, the scourge that is cancer, how death offers us all a chance to assess our own lives. It was an outpouring of love, a gathering that brought comfort to me and to many listeners around the country.

I've had a long love affair with radio. It is how I make my living and nothing is more fun. But it goes beyond that. Radio has provided me a chance to build a legacy, to make a tiny bit of difference in the lives of some, many of them strangers. I consider it an honor.

As of this writing, I am still working on air at WBZ but in a different capacity, as host/producer of several pre-recorded features, which I've been doing happily for four years. Sadly, like all things, the all-night radio show had to end. But it was my decision to end it, extremely rare in this business as you have read. Here's how it happened:

In May of 2016, just before I was to get remarried to a wonderful lady, I had an honest to goodness epiphany, the kind that happens in a Frank Capra film. Roberta and I were in Florida to attend a friend's daughter's wedding, a month prior to our own nuptials. We had just come from a cocktail party on the eve of that out-of-state wedding, when we decided to stop for something to eat. After ordering pizza, I put down my water glass and said to her, "You know, I believe it's time to go." Roberta looked up and said, "We just got here." Then she nervously added, "Oh no, what are you saying, you don't want to get married now?" I assured her everything with us was better than fine. "What do you mean then, it's time to go?" she asked again, anxious to hear the answer. I said, "Roberta, I'm thinking it's time to call it quits, to stop doing the radio show on the weekends."

At first, she thought I had lost it; Roberta knew how much I loved doing the show on WBZ. But with the upcoming marriage and me about to turn 58, it suddenly became clear that I needed and wanted more time for life. I was itching to have weekends free, (I had been working weekends since my early teens as a busboy). I wanted to only take naps when I felt like it, if I felt like it. It was time to explore the notion of regular sleep. People raved about it. The amount of prep work I did for the show was extensive, probably fifteen to twenty hours a

174

week. There were other projects and adventures I was looking to tackle. And the sense of accomplishment was real. Over 10,000 hours logged, thousands of guests and topics, hundreds of thousands raised for Boston Children's Hospital and long lasting relationships with listeners, guests, and colleagues.

Roberta supported my decision but suggested I wait till the following week when we returned to Boston to allow me time to think it over a bit. I did wait, but only until Tuesday morning of the following week when I made an appointment to see Peter Casey. We had a warm conversation in which I told him my plan and that I would work for at least the next six weeks, looking to wrap things up after the July 4th weekend, when I would host my final Boston Pops Show. Peter is such a gentleman. He agreed with my decision and told me how much I meant to WBZ, thanking me for my many contributions. He remains a dear friend.

I announced all of this to the audience a few weeks before "retiring." So many people were supportive, sad to see me go, but excited for me and grateful for the show I brought them over the years. The adrenaline was pumping during that final broadcast. Folks from all over, including some of my favorite regular callers and guests called in, sharing many memories and much laughter. The final sign off, a ritual in radio that I had performed thousands of times, was just five minutes away at 3:25am. It felt like a NASA launch countdown. I had a few words written out but scrapped those seconds before. I thanked everyone for their love and support and kindness over the years, reminded them that even though I was leaving the show, I would still have a presence on the station and planned to keep up with my voice-over work and community projects. As was my wish, I thought the occasion merited music to roll under my words. I chose an instrumental version of my favorite song, "Pure Imagination," from *Willy Wonka and the Chocolate Factory*. The lyrics, sung by the incomparable Gene Wilder always touched my heart. AS the song suggested, if you want to change the world, imagination offers a fine pathway.

With a minute left of the Jordan Rich Show, I broke up, tears flowing, voice cracking. I never felt more alive. The song ended. Radio had been and continues to be a world of pure imagination for me, my "Golden Ticket." And the fun hasn't stopped.

CHAPTER EIGHT
Is Anyone Listening?

As I sit typing this chapter in the summer of 2020, it's interesting to note that the first official radio broadcast occurred nearly 100 years ago. It was a radio news program airing August 31, 1920 over station 8MK in Detroit, Michigan. The station has lasted for a century and exists today as the powerful all-news radio station WWJ.

Over the past 100 years, radio has evolved in numerous ways. But throughout that evolution, there have been important constants. Radio has always maintained the ability to form an emotional bond with listeners. In the 1930s and 1940s it made us laugh with the likes of George Burns & Gracie Allen, Bob Hope, Edgar Bergen, Amos 'n' Andy, Jack Benny, Eddie Cantor, Red Skelton and others. Audiences were glued to their sets to hear Mel Allen or Red Barber call ballgames, letting us in on The Babe's latest homerun feat or Dizzy Dean's prowess with the fastball. Millions huddled around their living room console radios to catch the latest ringside boxing matches. Radio became part of the national fabric. We were grateful to

Walter Winchell, Lowell Thomas and Edward R. Murrow for keeping us informed of national and world events. Radio dramas brought us adventure and escape *("Look, up in the sky, it's a bird, it's a plane...")*, while a few scared the hell out of us, leading to panic (1938's *The War of the Worlds* broadcast, produced and hosted by Orson Welles). Throughout the Great Depression and World War II, President Roosevelt's fireside chats reassured the country during times of great stress. The 1930s and 40s brought live coverage of the big bands from big city downtown hotel ballrooms thrilling audiences with the music of Glenn Miller, Benny Goodman, Lionel Hampton, Duke Ellington and so many more. With television still some years away, radio was by far the number one medium for entertainment, information and a sense of connection.

In the 1950s radios got smaller as the sound got bigger with personalities like Alan Freed and Dick Clark introducing Rock n' Roll to a post-World War II generation. We were soon listening to transistor radios the size of cigarette packs, many of them imported from Japan, a nation that just a short time earlier nearly fought us to the death. By 1951, 50% of all cars had a radio; by 1965 the number jumped to 80%. In the late-1960s FM radio debuted and the way we listened to radio changed again. No longer relegated to playing the top hits of the day over and over in Top-40 fashion, FM stations went the way of "deep album cuts" with several forms of alternative programming with free form formats taking hold. In the 1970s and 1980s radios began to grow again in actual size as Boom Boxes became the rage, sharing the market with the ever-popular Walkman players that enabled us to take radio with us on foot. On air formats, delivery and content continued to evolve. By the 1990s and early-2000s, shock-jock radio drew a new line in the "standards" sand with personalities such as Howard Stern and Don Imus loading the industry with controversial content. There were many imitators, not all of them successful. What was considered off limits on radio soon became acceptable on many outlets. It was also around this time that technology gobbled up radio and spit it back out onto phones, computers and tablets. We could now receive traditional broadcast signals in a variety of new digitally superior ways, including the most popular girl in many American households, "Alexa." And let's not forget about the introduction of satellite radio, which few took 'Sirius' at the time (sorry about that). Who was ever going to pay for something that all along had been free over the public airwaves?

We doubters said the very same things about pay TV.

Oops!

Radio has had an exciting history for 100 years now and yours truly has played a tiny role in it for about 50% of that time. A decent run that I hope to continue. People ask what being in the radio business is like. There is surely the art and fun of doing it. But a key part of the answer is that radio is first a business. And the most significant transition in the business of radio has been deregulation.

Radio changed drastically in 1996, the year Washington deregulated radio, opening the floodgates for corporate consolidation, and by most accounts, the death of local community broadcasting. The idea was that instead of having five stations fighting for ad dollars in one market, it was fiscally more advantageous to have fewer stations, perhaps only two, going head-to-head. Some believed that allowing a single radio group to gain 40-50% of region share would help radio better compete in the overall media marketplace. It was strongly suggested that flush with higher ad revenues, radio clusters would invest more dollars to develop community programming, while propping up their on-air talent or, at the very least, attracting first-rate on-air talent from other markets.

180

Unfortunately, while most of the corporate conglomerates took advantage of the reduced competition to bring in more ad money, they didn't reinvest as predicted. Homogenization became the rule. Fewer on-air announcers were needed when a company could flip to automation. Deregulation led to the disappearance of long popular local on-air personalities, the rise of computer-programmed playlists, and more syndicated programming. In essence, it swallowed up many local stations, with others on life-support.

WBZ is, to a certain extent, one of the few holdouts to present live local programming nearly all week, day and night. Turn on WBZ radio at 3:00am and you will hear a news anchor, meteorologist and traffic reporter with the latest local updates. Up until recently (The Covid-19 pandemic caused changes in so many formats including WBZ) live in-studio talk hosts manned my old shift during the late-night hours. Nearly all other stations in the market and across the country were airing generic national shows with nothing originating locally during those times. Sadly, there are fewer local stations serving their audiences. Now, there are some local warriors around the country who still sign on their stations to do what they always have—broadcasting in their public's interest, convenience and necessity. One nearby standout is WATD in Marshfield, Massachusetts, a southern suburb of Boston. It is owned and operated by Ed Perry, a longtime engineer who has assembled his share of transmitters and tower arrays. Ed and his staff have won numerous awards for local news coverage over the years. The station still does remotes, hires solid young talent from the area and is a welcome friend and partner to the many businesses and non-profits it serves. I tip my headphones in appreciation to Ed and other pioneering broadcasters still going it alone. They prove it can still be done.

Another sweeping change involves exciting technology breakthroughs that have led to "streaming" audio digitally. The fear was that the on-line listening experience would see people abandoning radio. While we did stop the manufacture and purchase of table tops, portables, transistors and consoles, we never stopped listening to radio. In fact, radio gained new listeners as it became more accessible in pristine digital clarity whenever we wanted it. Technology brought multiple benefits. First for the consumer, it meant a huge variety of options, the chance to listen to any station from anywhere on the planet. Far cry from me as a kid trying to tune my tiny transistor in hopes of catching a skip wave from Chicago or Cleveland. This helped put a ton of radio stations on an equal playing field. With all signals balanced in power on the digital spectrum, the lesser radio players saw new life again.

Part of the digital revolution was the welcome addition of podcasting that forwarded the concept of radio-on-demand. More on podcasting in a bit, but it's impressive to see how radio stations have adopted the use of podcasts to maintain and gain more listeners.

It's hard not to notice that nowadays fewer people actually listen to the radio *on the radio*, even in the car. Sure, many still listen to a ballgame, traffic reports, music or local talk the traditional way through their AM-FM dashboard models, but for others, it's either a stack of favorite CD's (and even those are becoming passé) or the impressive Bluetooth system, delivering audio on demand to your vehicle or iPhone with near perfect clarity. To the average human under 35, an actual radio might be something found at the Smithsonian, in a display case next to wrist watches, fax machines, and Mr. Coffee. Radio is alive and well thanks to the technology and delivery systems that for now are tough to beat. Who remembers static?

Another major change involves the overall content in mass media. With the rise of infotainment, we are subjected to much more opinion, innuendo and rumor than objective coverage. And it's no longer just the salacious stuff of Hollywood and Rock n' Roll. Television news is slanted in less than subtle ways, with partisanship edging out fairness nearly everywhere. Whether it's politics, sports, lifestyle, religion or the economy, there are few places on the TV dial where you'll find a reasonable sense of balance. Radio news, an area I've worked in now for decades, is less flashy and more intent on sharing the information quickly and efficiently. It doesn't mean biases don't creep in. Radio presents listeners with the main thrust of a story, important takeaways, items you need to know quickly, as opposed to the endless "analysis" usually skewed in one direction on cable news networks. On the radio, the talk show hosts take care of the opinion part; not so the news anchors.

Returning to the impact of the Internet, with the introduction of streaming capabilities, my show went from a regional, nearly national broadcast with a powerful over-the-air nighttime signal, to a program available everywhere on earth. Suddenly I was getting calls and emails from Alaska, Argentina, New Zealand and the UK. The Internet shrunk the world and radio jumped in to once again bring connection, this time to the world. Was it cool? You bet. Sending a WBZ T-shirt to a young listener in the Ukraine, hearing from fans in Hawaii, simulcasting my show with a presenter for the BBC in London—just a few of the terrific moments that technology opened up for us. Like so many, I was a Luddite who needed time to figure out this new world. I remember prepping in the newsroom for an early show in 1997, and my producer said, "You have to check this out. It's really helpful. You can get answers to any question you type into Yahoo." And I said, "Yahoo? Isn't that like chocolate milk or something?" I knew nothing of search engines, had barely gotten the hang of email. But there it was, Yahoo, the grand oracle of knowledge, at least until Google came along.

On a sadder note, what we have also witnessed, as I alluded to earlier, is the devaluing of the radio personality. Gone were so many of the disc jockeys who kept us company at the beach, before and after school, on the way to our jobs. Personality radio was reined in greatly or totally pushed aside in favor of exhaustively researched music formats (more music, much less talk) or outright syndication. It is always about the money. When radio management realized they could do what they do without having to pay as much for "talent," the die was cast.

This is why I'm grateful I have landed back in talk radio for the second half of my career. The music formats have become jukeboxes, with no future for talented broadcasters in my opinion. In talk radio, success is based mainly on the personality of the host. Thankfully I was allowed to be very much me. Personality is critical to developing an audience. I did a talk show with the help of a familiar persona – me. There was never a desire to fight with guests or listeners, or force the audience to listen to only my political views on an issue. Late nights were the perfect environment for a host like me. I probably wouldn't get a job at most talk stations today. They would turn me away saying, "He's not edgy or controversial enough." Fine with me. The inner satisfaction of being honest over the years has been worth it. The other reason a future as a local talk host is unlikely? Most of the talk shows you hear on radio today are syndicated. There are fewer local slots for broadcasters who live and work in their own community. That's the sad reality.

Anyone who knows me will tell you I am a gabber. I enjoy conversation and can start one with anyone—wait staff, cops, clergy, receptionists, kids, security guards, etc. The fact that I would make my living chatting it up with people, some of them world renowned celebrities, is pure kismet.

When I was a kid I listened to WEEI, which was a Boston talk radio station in the 1960s, with erudite and talented personalities whom I idolized, radio professionals such as Jim Westover, Howard Nelson, Len Lawrence, and Paul Benzaquin. They were eloquent, well read, courteous yet commanding. When I got into the business and had the chance to meet some of these veterans, it was like hanging outside the ballpark to meet my Red Sox heroes. I've befriended a lot of great radio and TV talents, inspiring, creative broadcasters with memorable voices who left their mark with audiences who never forgot them. So many were irreplaceable. For those of you from the New England area, names like these mean something—Larry Glick, Jess Cain, Betty Day, Gus Saunders, Jerry Goodwin, Natalie Jacobson, Dana Hersey, Sherm Feller, Jerry Williams, Rex Trailer, Tom Ellis, Ron Della Chiesa, Joe Martelle, and Ken Carter. Here in the Boston market one has to admire Matt Siegel, who has been the morning host at KISS-108 since 1981. That's more years than most of his audience has been alive. When he retires (and there's no indication it's coming anytime soon) nobody will truly replace him. He, like the others I've mentioned, has been a dependable voice forever. Listeners appreciate that. Well done Matt, I doubt there will be too many 40-year radio careers in the future.

Through all the changes, one thing remains intact. The Federal Communications Commission (FCC) watchdogs remain vigilant when it comes to what George Carlin called the "7 Words You Can't Say on Television." George, being an old Boston disc jockey, was certainly referring to radio as well. Sure, our on-air language has loosened up a bit with the times, and it's not uncommon to turn on sports talk radio and hear something like, "That pitcher sucked last night...he didn't have the balls to throw inside to a batter, and that pisses me off!" (Of course, if you're a native Bostonian you never use the word "pissa" without the adjective "wicked" before it. Here people "go down the Cape," "take a heart (haahhht) attack," and greet each other with the famously monosyllabic "howyadoin.") But I digress. Let one of the "dreaded seven" slip and the FCC will come at you and your license with pitchforks and torches.

With 40-plus years on radio, plying my craft 50 weeks per year, five to seven days a week, I estimate I've spent about 60,000 hours in front of a microphone. And I am proud to say that not once did I utter a career-threatening forbidden word. Certainly not intentionally. But there was that one time...

188

Those nasty words (and more have been added to Carlin's original list) are somewhere in the professional cortex (in a brain synapse folder called "Things Not to Do On Air-EVER!). I am not sure about other colleagues and how they deal with it, but I possess a well-worn inner switch that goes into super safety mode when that on-air light flashes. Call it professionalism based on muscle memory, it's there and it works. It also helps to have another man-made safety valve. I refer to the famous 10-second delay option in talk radio, there to protect the station from unsanctioned language, slander, libel charges, etc. Luckily for me, I've had the chance to work with several fine call screeners and producers, who develop an instinct for the job and know just when to initiate the "kill switch," the delay function. They're doing their job and paying attention, along with me, in upholding standards while protecting the license to broadcast.

Except for that one time. We all remember the infamous Janet Jackson wardrobe incident during the 2004 Super Bowl halftime show. The nation was shocked and outraged to catch a momentary glimpse of Janet's upper privates. In light of that embarrassing incident, the FCC greatly raised the penalties and fines for obscenity on TV networks and radio stations. So what does that have to do with me? Here's the story of the "one time."

About a month after Janet flashed the world, I was anchoring the Sunday night show on WBZ, interviewing a Dartmouth college professor who had just authored a book on how adults should talk with teenagers about sexuality. I thought it to be a reasonable topic with an author who had done adequate research on the subject. The intent was as always, to present the subject matter in a respectful, professional manner, to educate and entertain.

The producer assigned to me that evening was not quite with it and sadly was saddled with personal problems that involved substance abuse. I had worked with her for several weeks and for the most part things went smoothly. She wasn't in a good place on this particular evening when it turned out I *really* needed her to be on her game. My guest on the telephone, an austere academic with several books and research papers to his name, started out perfectly fine with a professional overview of the subject matter. Then about two questions (fifteen minutes) into the interview, bam! He starts referring to sexual positions and practices in quite the candid way, using street language teens might use, complete with some of those Carlin phrases verboten when the red light is on. He referenced the Clinton era and the "act" that was famously the denouement of the scandal. I cannot bring myself to write about it more explicitly. My mother will be reading this book. The meltdown took less than 60 seconds. The oblivious professor rambled on seemingly unaware about the fact that he was on a 50,000-watt clear channel radio station at the time. I shut my mic and desperately tried to get the producer's attention to initiate the delay switch to cut him off. Or at least to bring his live audio down, to cut him off. I waved frantically, bellowing over the internal intercom system. She was leaning back in her chair, ignoring my pleas, staring into space. I finally took the only action I could; cutting in on the professor in mid-sentence suggesting it was time for a commercial break. That direction she finally heard, we went to the break and I instructed her to tell the guest from the control room that the interview was over. But the damage was done. The words and descriptions were uttered. The thought of a major dustup with the FCC involving a huge potential fine (which would have been levied on the station and CBS Radio) meant a ton of trouble for the company, as well as a storm of trouble for me, possibly costing me my job. As it turns out there was nary a complaint. Because the guest was so professorial in tone, few if any noticed his choice of terms. Talk about hiding in plain sight! I dodged a big one.

The producer soon left the station for rehab. I never reported her misconduct to the managers. The next morning, I called the professor (whom I had spoken with at length when booking him) told him why we cut him and asked if he understood what trouble his actions might have caused. I swear, no lie, he thought nothing of what he was saying at the time, didn't seem to have any inkling that there was even an FCC. I also don't think he ever watched a Super Bowl halftime show. He did humbly apologize. I refrained from booking professors who wrote books about sex going forward. To quote *Seinfeld,* "Not that there's anything wrong with that."

Now, more about the advent of podcasting. The technology has enabled creative, passionate people to express themselves, delve into very specific niches, delivering radio's answer to TV and "audio on demand!" Unlike radio which is widely accessible, one has to seek out podcasts, which isn't necessarily a bad idea. Because of infinite space on the Internet cloud, there is ample room for any and all podcasters. Some, like me, are radio pros, others are hobbyists launching episodes from their kitchen tables. Plenty of room in the podcast pool. I for one am a fan of podcasts that cater to my interests, such as film, comedy, history and storytelling. I now make a living creating, producing and hosting podcasts, with at least a half dozen of my own including "On Mic with Jordan," "Late Night Classics with Jordan," (celebrity interviews from the WBZ archives), "The Upside with Jordan" (good news stories) and more. The timing couldn't have been better. I left WBZ in 2016 segueing quickly to podcasting which meant the chance to continue interviewing, telling stories, informing and entertaining. For me, podcasting has been an extension of all I love about radio.

Some say we'd never miss radio if it went the way of the dinosaurs. I disagree. Radio is a dependable ally for many reasons. When there's an emergency – weather, terrorism, pandemic - we need information promptly. Radio can deliver critical information efficiently and quickly. The 9/11 terror attacks are a prime example. WBZ went full on with reporters, talk hosts and producers covering a multitude of aspects from dozens of locations. Ratings skyrocketed, as they do during the winter season when weather plays a part in our lives. But it provides more than information in a timely manner. Radio is, and has always been, a familiar, comforting presence, a friend we can rely on to be there for us. The feedback from thousands of listeners over the years is proof enough to me of radio's impact.

My long-standing love affair with radio is still red hot. Certainly, the industry is evolving, as are so many things. As long as we have iPhones with the latest audio apps (and that technology is only going to keep advancing) we can still be loyal to our favorite stations. Until self-driving automobiles take over for good, we will stay connected to our dashboard radios or whatever they call the audio delivery systems at the time.

Finally, to quote Albert Einstein, "Logic will get you from A to Z; imagination will get you everywhere." Radio was once referred to as "theater of the mind," and despite the barrage of video and in-your-face imagery available today, the allure of imagination is very much alive and well. Two granddaughters of mine under the age of six confirm my hypothesis when they listen to their Papa read them stories and react with glee. Radio has a future as long as that of imagination and wonder.

CHAPTER NINE
Family Ties

I'm gonna be like you, dad"
"You know I'm gonna be like you"

Ah, a line from a classic song from my youth; and in many ways they reflect my life.

I've spent close to 50 years in radio, which means I've probably spent more time in front of a microphone than with family. Saying that aloud sounds a bit sad. Was I less than an attentive husband and father? Based on calendar entries, it would certainly appear that way. After all, I missed birthday parties, anniversaries and many family events because I was either on-air or working on extensive audio projects at Chart Productions. My first wife, Wendy, and I, were like two proverbial ships passing in the night; I'm arriving home, she's going to bed; she's waking up, I'm about to hit my pillow. Despite the challenges of a hectic schedule, we did arrange for quality time and managed to raise two beautiful children. Much of the credit, though, goes to Wendy. She was totally dedicated to motherhood and was there for a lot of things that I wasn't.

Some of us take for granted our partners for any number of reasons. I appreciate how much she allowed me to pursue career opportunities. At the same time, I regret not saying "no" enough to be where it counts—with family.

The last two lines of Chapin's song also own special meaning, as my son, Andrew, is currently working at WBZ as a producer, board operator and copywriter, following my lead into radio. An English and writing major in college, Andrew struggled, like a lot of recent grads, to find a job in the creative writing field. When I caught word of openings at WBZ, I suggested he look into it. He did and has proven to be a valuable member of the radio team. The neatest part of him working at the station is that for the final two years of my late-night talk show, Andrew served as the producer of "The Jordan Rich Show." Cue the bias alerts, he was the finest producer I ever had on the show. I would often invite him to hold calls and join me in the booth to converse about any number of subjects – television, film, pop culture, history. To my understanding, we were the only father-son team working on the same show together in Boston radio history. Maybe not Guinness Book worthy, but some of my happiest and proudest moments involve working with Andrew.

Here's what I know. As much as my career ambitions had an impact on the family, it was family that allowed me to achieve my goals, thanks to their unwavering support, love and encouragement. I've shared with you the story of my supportive parents who allowed me to pursue a life in the arts. Now, more about emerging as an adult and looking to start a family of my own.

It began at a singles dance in the spring of 1980 at the old Sheraton-Needham Hotel, high on a hill on Route 128, just west of Boston. The hotel, like so many other structures, was razed and rebuilt many years ago, just as the Boston hospital in which I was born was torn down after I arrived in 1958. Coincidence? That's open to debate.

During my early 20's, life was hectic with hosting weekend dances and parties as a DJ, as well as long hours spent getting Chart Productions up and running. Not much time for a social life, or the opportunity to seek out a date. Of course, there were females in my orbit in high school and college but none made it to "serious girlfriend" stage. By the time college was over I was under friendly pressure to get out and socialize. So I went, somewhat reluctantly, on a rare Saturday night off to an actual singles dance. Time for a little digression. This would be the

197

second singles event I had ever attended. The first resulted in me meeting an "older woman" (I was 20, she 28). We saw each other for a month or so. My parents were not keen on that relationship, to say the least. It was after all 40 years ago; today an age gap like that doesn't mean as much. I chose to break up with her when it seemed that things were moving a bit too quickly.

The young woman had a lot of things "figured out" for both of us in the short time we dated and I felt a chill coming on—time to make a graceful exit. When I arrived at her apartment to break up, as gently as possible, she thrust in my face a two-page letter filled with Jordan's direct quotes, nearly everything I had said to her, as if her apartment had been bugged. Nixon had nothing over her in-house taping system. Pillow talk apparently was not off limits and sure enough I waxed a bit romantically over the month, as is my style. Those "sweet nothings" came back to bite me. But I stood silent, took the scolding and the letter, wished her well and sped to the nearest Dunkin' Donuts, desperate for decaf. That was the sad story of singles dance number one.

Back to the second dance, the one that *really* counted. It was odd not spinning the records or emceeing a dance, but actually attending as a civilian. I felt out of place, looking over at the DJ and wondering about his playlist. There were a lot of women on the dance floor, outnumbering the men by a fair margin. But only one stood out. Her full name was Wendy Levine (I would only learn that much later) and she was a very attractive young woman, blonde with a bright smile. I assumed she was an officer of the group running the dance. She was dressed in a conservative navy-blue suit and had that look that suggested, "This girl has her it together!" I worked up the courage to ask her to dance and she agreed. We enjoyed one dance together (to Sinatra's "My Way"). As Old Blue Eyes reminded us 'that now, the end was near,' we parted ways. I wanted very much to see her again but realized I had no address or phone number. It was very pre-Internet and took me about a week to track her down.

We had our first real date at the Hampshire House across from the Public Gardens, the location used for the *Cheers* TV show. We spent a long time talking about a lot of things and realized we had a lot in common. What I loved was that she wasn't impressed to be dating a radio personality. At that time, I was working for WRKO as your dependable weather reporter, direct from the closet at Logan Airport. Honestly, I'm embarrassed when people get too excited about what I do.   Radio is my craft, passion, but it's also my job. I'm deserving of no more respect or admiration than anyone else who works hard. It has always been comforting to be accepted for who I am, not the person who graces the airwaves. Having interviewed hundreds of celebrities, I can empathize with the struggles some have with identity. I liked the fact that Wendy was not there for the performer, but for me. I would be lucky enough to find that very same dynamic in a future relationship.

But here's where the story of meeting Wendy involves a bit of kismet. A good friend of mine from college was also working at WRKO at the time. About a month before the singles dance, he showed me a letter that he received from a former summer camp friend, a sweet, thoughtful note saying how wonderful it was to hear him on the radio after so many years. I didn't give it much thought at the time, but remember saying to my buddy how nice it was for this girl to write him.   It really was touching.   Turns out it was Wendy who penned that endearing letter to my friend. A strange coincidence that we spoke about when we put two and two together the night of our first date. And here's another odd thing (cue the *Twilight Zone* theme). About a year earlier I was asked to do a speaking engagement at a summer camp in the city that catered to special needs children. As I arrived, there was a bit of commotion with the counselors looking a bit panicky. It seemed that one of the special needs youngsters had run off somewhere with his counselor heading off to find him. That special needs counselor who did eventually find the boy was none other than Wendy Levine. Apparently, we weren't destined to meet then. Life is indeed a series of random moments stitched together to make sense.

She was from Quincy and I was from Randolph, two South Shore kids. We got married in 1982. At the time Wendy was a special education teacher in Hudson, Massachusetts, so it made sense that we would live first in Natick and then in Framingham. Harkening back again to the last two lines of that Harry Chapin song; our first-born daughter, Lindsay, is a special education teacher in New York, just like her Mom.

Wendy was a strong, confident, outgoing woman. She was an only child who didn't suffer from that familiar syndrome that some without siblings do. Children without siblings are sometimes spoiled, antisocial or lonely. But not Wendy. It's one of the reasons I fell for her so quickly. She so often put others first, certainly me. Since the beginning she supported my work and the non-stop schedule I kept.

201

Soon after we were married, I was working in Lowell at WLLH, where I wouldn't get home until 10:00pm some nights. I'd be eating dinner while she's getting ready for bed. Those were challenging days, but we got through them and she rarely complained. In retrospect, I wish I had spent more time with her and later with the kids, especially on weekends. Like Sinatra, "Regrets, I've had a few." That was a big one.

Her support was there, even when the bottom fell out and I got fired from various radio jobs. Whereas some might take out their frustrations on their husbands, Wendy was much angrier at the station managers who let me go. She wanted to eviscerate them! I had to physically hold her back from calling certain unnamed radio execs who would have gotten a loud taste of what was on her mind! I've always lived with the wisdom of my mentor Roger Allan who reminded us to never, ever burn a bridge, especially in broadcasting with so much turnover. Fortunately, even during those employment setbacks, money was never an issue. She had a solid job and Chart Productions was humming along and providing a steady income.

My late first wife was all about motherhood, devoted 100% to our children. My respect for her and so many working moms is immense. She was working full time while doing much heavy-lifting when it came to the kids. So often I was elsewhere, rising at 3:00am, doing radio all day, interviewing celebrities, spinning records, introducing large purple dinosaurs. I poured into the work, burning many candles, being there when I could for the family. Sleep and socializing took a back seat to being engaged at home. I'm proud to have said "no" to a fair share of press openings and free dinners. Still, back then I wasn't smart enough to understand the importance of saying "no." It's something I've gotten better at as I've aged.

Weekends were the trickiest. During the week children have school and activities, and are busy so much of the time. But we lost a lot of weekends when they would have loved to have Dad around. It was a choice I made willingly, to grab opportunities as they came up. Because of the fun nature of the work, the kids would accompany me to the studio, theatre, fundraisers, etc. They even got a chance to appear on radio. Andrew and Lindsay were each no older than three and barely able to read when Dad would cast them in radio spots. I would feed them their lines and have them recite them back to me in tiny choruses into a recorder. It's fun to listen back to my now adult children who back then were adorable voice-over stars. Years later, I would bring Andrew with me to WBZ to "co-host" for awhile. At 12 he took to it like a natural. Now he's a qualified radio engineer, producing talk shows and writing the news at that very same station. He's also the host of his own podcast called "Music of the Mat," a deep dive into professional wrestling. He's done over 85 episodes and is a compelling host, and that's not just his old man talking. I read listener comments. Lindsay followed in her late Mom's footsteps and is teaching special education in New York City. She loves her work and her students, just as Wendy did.

I am very proud of my children for tons of reasons. They have accomplished much in their young lives. But they've also dealt with the pain of watching their mother lose a battle with cancer so early. It was certainly a tough stretch for us, as it is for any family. I suppose it was fortunate; the worst stages of the cancer occurred when Lindsay and Andrew were older, away in college or beyond. Friends and relatives would occasionally step in to help but I was effectively the sole caretaker for Wendy in the final year and a half of her life. Unsettling— no, horrifying as it was—we summoned the strength to somehow get up and keep going, resting our hopes on any slight chance that a clinical trial might buy us more time. It was an honor to be her caretaker, as a knight defends his maiden. But it was devastating knowing time was not on our side.

I was operating on autopilot during the last year as Wendy's health began to deteriorate. Our rabbi, by now a close personal friend, was there for us spiritually. The doctors, nurses, and hospice workers couldn't have done more for her. Hospice certainly deserves special praise. People who work in hospice care are the closest thing to angels on earth. They make the unthinkable more bearable. Before the end, Wendy and I talked about the future. I would try and change the subject, to find something else to discuss, but she was insistent we deal with it. Wendy insisted that Lindsay's wedding happen as planned. The date was set for mid-November. Wendy passed away in August of 2013, and was not here to see Lindsay walk down the aisle. Only one thing proved somewhat lucky for me. During the final months and beyond, I experienced no signs of depression. Just intense sadness and anger, how one should feel.

If you'll indulge me, here's one sweet story as to how my son dealt with his Mom's illness.

Wendy was very sick, thinning, frail and in pain during the final five months of her life. Andrew was home from college for spring break and his mother was understandably uncomfortable and cranky. She wasn't doing well. And Andrew, who's an introvert by nature, was more quiet than usual, locking himself away in his room for long stretches. He barely spoke more than a few words to either of us. Wendy was visibly upset about his being so aloof and seemingly un-interested in what was happening. Her ire about it got to me. These were stressful days and with my fuse rather short, it finally meant me confronting him. "What's the matter with you?" I said. "Don't you have any feelings at all about Mom? How can you be so uninvolved and uncaring?" I said things I quickly regretted in that outburst. A few hours later I apologized and came up with a suggestion, which might have been the wisest "Dad idea" I'd had in years. I said, "Andrew, why don't you write a letter to Mom about how you feel? You're a gifted writer and it might do Mom a world of good." By the end of that day, he did what I asked. He wrote about his feelings. I expected a paragraph or two. What he delivered was a single-spaced full-page letter expressing feelings for and about his mother, his fears, wishes and most of all, his love for her. Wendy was overwhelmed when she read it; we both cried. I treasure a copy of that letter to this day.

Wendy's death closed a major chapter. We were together 33 years, had built a life, a family, a foundation. But as is often the case, the closing of a window leads to an opening of others. A new window would open the following summer.

I was alone in the house in Framingham wrapping up the necessary paperwork, donations, and acknowledging friends and family for their support and messages of sympathy. When the activity that follows a death slowed, I began thinking of a future. Despite the fact that I'm surrounded by many in my professional life, I felt a void in not having someone to spend time with. Sadness over our loss will always be with me. But it was loneliness that settled in as 2014 arrived. So I did something that I never thought in a million years I would do; I signed up with an online dating service.

One would think in the glamorous world of major market broadcasting, there would be many opportunities to meet single women. Not necessarily the case. Nearly everyone I knew was married or attached, which was fine. The prospect of going to dances or trying to meet someone at a bar was unappealing. I had not done the dating thing for decades which is why computer matching made sense. What did I have to lose?

After signing up and preparing my profile, I was ready to initiate. Just forgot one minor detail; in a silly attempt to protect my identity, I didn't upload any photos. Huh? How would one expect to garner any interest with a blank silhouette where the photo should have been? I thought about a listener or two or 20 spreading the news that the radio guy was now on the dating circuit. Little did I realize that the chance of even getting a "nibble" was slim without proof of life in the form of a headshot. But luck and the fates intervened and sight unseen, I got a response.

It didn't take long to find someone with a series of attractive photos and a stunning profile. This woman liked people for who they were, not what they owned. She loved Italian food and chocolate, enjoyed many other things I do and was obviously bright, comfortable, and confident. I thought, "Hmm, intriguing. But would she be at all interested in meeting someone like me?" So I emailed her through the site (neither of us using our real names of course) and she responded, "I am replying because it's the courteous thing to do when someone pings me." She added, "I have to ask, are you either in the witness protection program or do you look like Quasimodo? What's with no picture?" This lady had a keen sense of humor. A key ingredient.

I sent her my phone number and hoped she'd call. Sure enough she did. I told her why I didn't include a photo. Then I asked her to call up my website, which featured a variety of photos proving my existence. She told me later that she listened to a podcast on the site for additional confirmation. Wise woman. The vetting process worked. We decided to meet the following Monday for lunch, which happened to be Memorial Day.

We ended up on our first meeting at the only spot open for lunch on the holiday, a Brazilian steakhouse near the Westin Hotel in Copley Square. I arrived a few minutes early and there stood Roberta, an early arrival herself. This was my first date in 34 years and I was rather nervous. As soon as we shook hands, she looked down and noticed something. She said, "Are you sure you want to do this? You're still wearing your wedding ring." She knew I was widowed, but felt that the wedding ring suggested I was not ready to move on. I stammered for a second, insisting I was indeed ready, that it had been a long slow goodbye with my late wife over the last few years. That's how our relationship began, with direct honest talk. We ended up enjoying a three-hour lunch, "eating a zoo," as Roberta recalls. I left thinking this was a woman I would like to get to know, she was beautiful, active, confident, and age appropriate. As I headed to my car, watching her walk in the other direction to the South End of Boston, I thought, "That went well. Hopefully there will be another opportunity to see her."

I called her the next day and we made another date. She had tickets to the Red Sox game at Fenway Park and invited me to join her. I said, "Great, let me take you out to lunch beforehand!" Lunch was near the ballpark. We then went to Fenway and in JR fashion I had to leave the game in the seventh inning with the Red Sox leading, to host a charity event, of course. Roberta said no problem. I thought, if she's going to put up with me flying the coop on date two, then she would be worth pursuing. She confessed to me shortly thereafter, that had I showed up again wearing the wedding ring it would have been our last date. She had been hurt in the past by others who weren't ready, sincere or committed. I totally understood and respected her for feeling that way. Incidentally, I had removed the ring after the Memorial Day lunch. It remains a treasured reminder of another life, with me always..

We continued to date, I wooed Roberta in many corny ways, and after a year I proposed. The proposal was quite the affair, with me dressed in a full penguin body suit (she nicknamed me

210

'her penguin' months earlier) in a neighborhood family diner that we frequented, complete with serenading singers and a restaurant full of supporters. We married in June of 2016. Meeting Roberta brought love into my life for a second time, making me quite the lucky man.

Roberta comes from a large nuclear and extended family. My clan would barely fill a booth at the IHop. She's from Brookline, Massachusetts, a big city when you compare it to my hometown of Randolph. Radio defined my life; Roberta didn't even know where WBZ was on the dial. This made her perhaps the one person in New England not to have WBZ ingrained in her DNA. Obviously, she never cared much about snow days with WBZ's legendary Gary LaPierre rattling off no-school announcements. Turns out she doesn't listen to radio much because—wait for it—she prefers music over talk (uh-oh). We had been dating for six weeks before Roberta ever heard me on the radio. She was driving on the way to dinner with a friend. This friend asked her if she was seeing anyone special at that time, and Roberta tells her of a guy named Jordan Rich. It turns out that her friend, Kate, was one of my fans. She says to Roberta, "Have you heard him on the radio?" Roberta says, "No, I don't stay up that late." Kate tells her they can listen to him right now in prime time because he's about to do the 4th of July broadcast from the Charles River Esplanade. So they turn on the radio and there I am. Roberta calls me while I'm doing the show to say, "Hey, we're listening. And you know, you sound pretty good." A resounding endorsement. But that's Roberta, telling it like it is, and that's why I love her.

George Bernard Shaw once said "A happy family is but an earlier heaven." Old George was on to something. I could not have succeeded, persevered or overcome pain and challenge without the love and support of family. My blessings extend to very close friends who are as dear to me as any brothers and sisters could be. And those blessings keep on coming with the arrival of two darling granddaughters and a very special niece. Life is good.

CHAPTER TEN

What a Long, Strange (But Interesting) Trip It's Been

Upon its publication, it is inevitable that someone will ask, "Why did you decide to write a book?"

But what they might *really* be thinking, but are far too polite to say, is "C'mon, why do you think your life is so interesting that people will actually want to plunk down $10.95 to read your story?" It's a reasonable question, one that I find easy to answer. I don't believe I'm that interesting. In fact, my life has been remarkably ordinary, which is just the way I like it. No brushes with the long arm of the law, no embarrassing public scandals, certainly no death-defying exploits or heroic moments to crow about. Nope, I'm just a guy living a quiet life taken up with family, friends and work. I'll grant you, the work that I do is not exactly "quiet" and what I do might be interesting to some. I didn't undertake this writing project to pump up my image or oversell my accomplishments. The listening public is the best arbiter of what I've accomplished in my chosen profession. I've never held to the belief that success is measured by income, status or ratings alone. It has been and always shall be about making a difference, however slight, in the lives of others.

We write for different reasons. I chose this format (short memoir) as a response to my subconscious (that of a well-modulated, trained announcer voice that still resides in my cranium), my inner narrator who nagged me to do this as a gift to my grandchildren. And it has been a highly rewarding experience, a chance to tell a tale while acknowledging the many who have helped me grow and learn, both on and off-air. It has been a cathartic undertaking that has helped me tend to wounds and heal by sharing. The project has served as self-examination, a thank you, a chance to impart a bit of wisdom. Of course, I'll be honored if others, besides blood relatives, read it. What I've offered is a peek behind the curtain of local radio, with its highs and lows for this particular performer and, yes, the magic it still holds for me. Radio and culture have changed much during the last four decades. I've grown up in the midst of it all and have learned a few things. The main one is that through it all, broadcasters continue to be entrusted with something sacred—a connection to people, a population of disparate souls, every one unique, all members of the radio audience.

Stephen King once boasted that he writes every day of the year except for his birthday and Christmas. Talk about discipline. I admire the tenacity of professional authors, certainly after slogging through my 10 chapters for the six months it took to complete, all while working full-time at Chart Productions and producing features and podcasts for WBZ Radio. Much of this project has occurred during the defining event of our times, the Covid-19 pandemic. Probably as good a time as any to be home attacking the keyboard. What helped was the suggestion by my editor Steve White, who advised tackling things in chronological order, one chapter at a time. Simple enough and it worked for me. Steve's expertise, guidance and patience were so helpful. As a radio man for whom following a format is second nature, proceeding in linear fashion made the process flow smoothly. As time consuming and daunting as it has been, I'm very happy to have done it. And for anyone out there considering writing their own story, what are you waiting for? Even if it never leaves the confines of your laptop, you'll reap many inner benefits; someday your family will thank you for it.

A few notes about the process. My initial thought was, "Oy, how am I going to remember details from over the past 40 years?" Once I began writing, the memory banks started clicking and details began to re-emerge. Interestingly enough, the chapters that came most easily were the ones that dealt with the more serious issues, namely my encounters with depression and Wendy's death. Catharsis made a difference (it's quite real) and provided me with the energy to continue. I certainly enjoyed recalling and writing about the good times, the humor, the friendships, mentors and personalities that have been my touchstones. And then of course there are my listeners, whom I appreciate today more than ever. I sifted through old photo albums, scripts, newspaper clippings, classic WRKO and WSSH playlists and old radio air-checks. My voice was higher back in 1979, with my regional "Bahstan" accent far from tamed. Listening to tapes from decades ago only confirms the old axiom "that you're only as good as your last broadcast." Artists should always look to better something in their performance each and every day. I also spoke with long standing colleagues to help fill in any certain blank spots. Thanks to them all. Writing about yourself requires detective work. Playing Sherlock has been lots of fun.

This project also reminded me that I've packed a lot into this life, not all of it great, but much of it interesting. Writing helped me appreciate the many opportunities that have come my way. It also broadened my gratitude and understanding of a broadcaster's responsibility, that it's an honor and privilege to be in the business, playing a vital role in the lives of the public.

Before signing off, let me offer you my short list of life lessons, some inspired by the mentors I've told you about, others honed by yours truly in the logging of thousands of on air hours.

1.   Never think you matter more than the engineer who built the transmitter. Being a broadcaster makes you no more special than the cleaning lady, the security guard, the usher or the plumber. Besides, the plumber likely makes more per hour.

2.   Be respectful of everyone—your loved ones, colleagues, friends, dentists—and if you're getting into my business, pay special attention to respecting your audience.

3.   You know what a bridge is? Never ever burn one on the way out the door. In radio, chances are you'll be up for a job next month and that same dude who canned you will be waiting at the new place. A few months later, you could be the boss with that same dude knocking on *your* door.

4.   Screwing up on-air is the same as making a mistake anywhere else. Except that in radio, thousands will hear it. Guess what? If they notice at all, they'll forgive and forget. You're only a human with amplification. Relax.

5.   Best advice I ever got? "Do show prep!" I hated doing homework in school. Love doing it now as a grown-up broadcaster. Being prepared makes playing without a net (broadcasting live in front of thousands) quite manageable.

6.   Don't *ever* be afraid to ask for help. This is a biggie. Sucking it up and acting like a tough guy works only in the movies. We all need others to help us steady our gait, to be there when we fall. It's not a character flaw to have flaws. Help is available. Do the brave thing and ask for it.

7.   The most important skillset in radio is not diaphragmatic breathing, enunciation or reading copy— it's listening.

8.   The best salve for what ails us is humor. But it's a powerful elixir that on the public airwaves should be handled with care. My brand of humor comes in a tube labeled "self-deprecating – no end date." I use it as often as possible with excellent results.

9.   Take care of yourself. Find time to rest, get a good night's sleep, exercise, drink tea and eat healthy. But always: LEAVE ROOM FOR DESSERT.

10.   Routinely, at least once a year, watch *It's a Wonderful Life*, the 1946 classic starring Jimmy Stewart. When you realize we're all just like George Bailey, a lot of stuff will make sense to you.

I have two beautiful granddaughters, Elle and Carter, and a lovely niece Ella, all five and under.

What they know of their Papa (aka Uncle Jordan) is he's one heck of a playmate, ready to roll up his sleeves for any game or activity they can think up. *And standing by to spoil them at every turn.* Since I make a living telling stories, I offer this tale about me that I hope will explain a few things and inspire them to pursue their own dreams.

It's true, hard work always pays off. And remember, ladies, don't let anyone talk you out of doing what you love.

I laughed 15 or so years ago when Tom Brady of the Super Bowl Champion New England Patriots penned his biography at 25! Granted, it's Tom Brady, but surely there had to be more to his story than the first 25 years? In number 12's case there most certainly was.

There's a lot more to my story and much of it will involve this long-running love affair with this most magical of mediums. May others be as blessed to enjoy whatever they do in life as much as I have.

Until we meet again, I'll hit you with my standard sign-off that has been my friendly signature for decades. This is Jordan Rich reminding you to "Be well, so you can do good."

Peace.

APPENDIX

Some of the more than 150 people I have had the pleasure of talking with over the years.

ACTORS

Danny Aiello

Ed Asner

John Astin

Ed Begley Jr

Robbie Benson

Elizabeth Berkley

Theodore Bickel

Gerard Butler

Dyan Cannon

Robert Conrad

Kirk Douglas

Fran Drescher

Charles Durning

Barbara Eden

Chris Elliot

Robert Englund

Linda Evans

Mike Farrell

Carrie Fisher

June Foray

Ben Gazzara

Anita Gillette

Frank Gorshin

Linda Hamilton

Valerie Harper

Rex Harrison

Terri Hatcher

Mariel Hemingway

Lance Henriksen

Charlton Heston

Timothy Hutton

Shirley Jones

Cherry Jones

Gabe Kaplan

Stacey Keach

Eartha Kitt

Walter Koenig

Hugh Laurie

Hal Linden

Patti Lupone

Joe Mantegna

Lee Meriwether

Liza Minelli

Roger Moore

Kate Mulgrew

Bob Newhart

Leonard Nimoy

James Edward Olmos

Simon Pegg

Anthony Quinn

Tony Randall

John Ratzenberger

Debbie Reynolds

Cathy Rigby

Chita Rivera

Wayne Rogers

Mickey Rooney

Katherine Ross

William Schallert

Roy Scheider

Kyra Sedgewick

William Shatner

Harry Shearer

Cybil Shephard

Gary Sinise

Kevin Smith

Paul Sorvino

Arnold Stang

Lily Tomlin

Dick Van Dyke

Joyce Van Patten

Adam West

Rachel York

FUNNY PEOPLE

Marty Allen

Richard Belzer

Wayne Brady

George Carlin

Dick Cavett

Tim Conway

Pat Cooper

Dave Coulier

Bill Dana

Phyllis Diller

Jeff Dunham

Judy Gold

Chance Langton

Denis Leary

Bob Newhart

Jim Norton

Paula Poundstone

Colin Quinn

Carl Reiner

Don Rickles

Joan Rivers

Steve Sweeney

Steven Wright

MUSICIANS/SINGERS

Ian Anderson

Frankie Avalon

Count Basie

Jon "Bowzer" Bauman

Tony Bennett

Ann Hampton Calloway

Roseanne Cash

Freddy Cole

Paula Cole

Judy Collins

Jimmy Dean

Mercer Ellington

David Foster

Peter Frampton

Connie Francis

Kenny G

Buddy Guy

Rupert Holmes

Janis Ian

James Levine

Kenny Loggins

Mike Love

Nick Lowe

Melissa Manchester
Wynton Marsalis

Johnny Mathis

Marie Osmond

John Pizzarelli

Andre Previn

Herb Reed

LeAnn Rimes

Kenny Rogers

Tom Rush

Diane Schuur

Neil Sedaka

Mavis Staples

Livingston Taylor

Mel Torme

Bobby Vee

AUTHORS AND NOTABLES

Madeline Albright

Buzz Aldrin

Maya Angelou

Richard Bach

Ben Bova

Ray Bradbury

Senator Edward Brooke

Max Brooks

Orson Scott Card

Arthur C. Clark

Robin Cook

Richard Ben Cramer

Nelson DeMille

Duchess Sara Ferguson

William Gibson

Doris Kearns Goodwin

Sue Grafton

Brian Greene

Pete Hamill

Ray Harryhausen

Lauren Hillenbrand

Penn Jillette

Roger Kahn

Michio Kaku

Garrison Keillor

Caroline Kennedy

Ed Koch

Dean Koontz

The Amazing Kreskin

Ray Kurzweil

Errol Morris

Cousin Bruce Morrow

Dean Ornish

Gary Owens

Matthew Pearl

Ann Rule

Nicholas Sparks

R L Stine

Gay Talese

Calvin Trillin

Mike Wallace

Jerry Weintraub

About Stephen A. White

Stephen A. White grew up in South Boston and has been a writer for over 45 years, covering all facets of entertainment, business and popular culture. As a concert promoter he worked with some of the biggest names in music, and has interviewed close to 100 musical performers and actors and actresses, and has produced and hosted a 1960s radio show. Stephen is the owner of Steve White Public Relations, where he gets to put his writing skills to use helping companies maximize their marketing.

He is also the author of the 1960s novel *Time Passages* and has explored 1960s pop culture in his book, *American Pop,* both available on Amazon. Stephen has also been an editor, writer and publisher of many of his client's books. He lives in Hanover, MA with his wife, Claire, faithful rescue dog, Bella, and his collection of 1,400 CDs.

www.SteveWhitePublishing.com

Made in United States
North Haven, CT
20 March 2022

17369775R00127